An Anglican
Catechism

An Anglican Catechism

EDWARD NORMAN

CONTINUUM

London and New York

Continuum

The Tower Building

11 York Road

London SE1 7NX

370 Lexington Avenue

New York NY 10017-6503

British Library Cataloguing-in-Publication Data

A catalogue record for this book is available from the British
Library.

0 8264 5451 8

Typeset by YHT Ltd, London

Printed and bound in Great Britain by Biddles Ltd, Guildford and
King's Lynn

Contents

Foreword

by

The Most Reverend & Right Honourable David Hope
Archbishop of York

Down the centuries, the Church has felt it right to draw up schema of instruction which have reflected the perceived needs of its day. Luther's *Kleiner Katechismus* of 1529, the so-called *Penny Catechism* of 1898, not to mention, of course, our own Prayer Book Catechism and its 1961 Revision, are but some amongst the many. In setting his hand to this *Anglican Catechism*, Edward Norman stands, therefore, in a time-honoured tradition.

And yet, what he has produced could not be further from that rigid 'Question and Answer' format of former times. Despite that – indeed, perhaps because of it – he stands closer to the comprehensive spirit of Anglicanism. That spirit which, eschewing the rigidities of the confessional approach, prefers the broader freedoms which are delimited only by scripture, reason and tradition.

He sets out the doctrinal basis of the Christian faith – God, the Holy Trinity, Creation, Revelation, Sanctification – all the great themes are there – the underlying basis of Christian faith and Christian discipleship in every age.

It is in the context of this unchanging doctrinal basis of faith, and its engagement with a rapidly changing world, and in an Anglican context, that Edward Norman explores the very relevant issues for today – the economic and social order, warfare, human rights, sexual morality, and so on. To explore the implications of living out our faith in such a world needs the sort of signposting which is as sensitive and perceptive as it is clear and unambiguous.

It is with great pleasure that I commend this volume – a work more a celebration of Christian living than it is 'catechism'. It will surely provoke the reader to search for more – more deeply into the truth of things, more deeply into the heart of God as revealed in Jesus Christ.

I believe that his readers will be hugely grateful that Canon Norman has been able to offer them exactly this.

✠ David Ebor

Preface

This account of the teachings of Christianity as received within the Church of England is in no sense an official document. It began with an invitation from His Grace the Archbishop of York, Dr David Hope, to devise a scheme of training for lay and ordained ministry in the Diocese of York. At a very early stage in this work, however, it became apparent that some kind of statement or account of what the Church of England teaches would be an almost essential preliminary for any useful ministerial preparation — in conditions, such as those now common in our society, where understanding has been clouded by the prevalence of secular modes of thought, where there has been an immense expansion of knowledge and of access to it, and where the existence (as always in church history) of differences of interpretation and emphasis are present among Christian believers themselves. It also seemed suitable, from the beginning, to attempt a statement of the faith which had a wider purpose: to produce something which could be put into the hands of anyone seeking to know what the Church teaches, and to combine informal summaries with interpretive commentary. *The Alternative Service Book of the Church of England* (1980), and *Common Worship* (2000) do not contain catechisms, and the version in the Prayer Book is a brief inquisitorial text, plainly intended for use in a pre-literate age. Since this work was completed, the Church has announced that it has decided to produce a new catechism, and this will doubtless in due time appear. The catechism here follows the structure of the catechism of St Pius V (1566), and of the catechism promulgated in 1992 and produced by a Commission presided over by Cardinal Joseph Ratzinger, only in starting with the means by which religious knowledge is available to humanity.

Thereafter it separates from the four-part form in order to consider the teaching of the Church under the heads of doctrine, morals, and applications. I have consulted no one in producing this statement; any errors of interpretation or misunderstandings of fact, therefore, can only be attributed to me. I have also attempted to avoid offering alternative understandings. The Anglican tradition is richly endowed with differences of opinion, seemingly about even the most basic truths: the present statement aspires to be neither a comprehension nor a summary of these, but an accessible guide to what the mind of the Church of England has, in the perspective of centuries, considered the essentials of the teaching of Christ. As such this work may be useful to Christians of many traditions.

Edward Norman
York: April 2000

I

Doctrine and Order

THE HOLY TRINITY

God can be defined variously: in terms of his complete universality, his omniscience, his creative power, his preparedness to disclose himself through the evidences of his works, and through revelation. Of the last, humanity has been admitted to three forms, although undoubtedly God can be taken to exist in an infinite number of ways unknowable by men and women. As creatures, the normal condition of human life is to experience his worldly order; creatures are inseparable from creation and their vision of the Creator restricts him, so to say, to the limits of their worldly perception and under-

1

standing. Hence the phenomenon, which puzzles many, that God does not appear with immediacy in the world of our senses; he is not visible. The reverse of the present arrangement of things should be considered: if God was visible he would be the autocrat of the world, known in direct applications of sovereignty. He has chosen, instead, to allow free will and reason to men and women, and for that it is necessary for his sovereignty over humanity to be exercised indirectly. Men and women discover the values he decrees as the purpose of their existence through the education provided by choices available in daily living. Endowed with the capacity for higher reflection they can proceed then to an appreciation of those aspects of the divine nature which God disposes in his creation. God is not humanized by being conceived in limited terms; it is humanity which now sees through a glass darkly but will eventually receive a fuller understanding. Christ's promise of eternal life is of a life which has eternal (or durable) qualities; which begins in the world among those who submit to the divine will, and is completed among the company of the blessed to which those come, after death, who have loved God with all their heart.

Of the infinite number of ways in which God could disclose himself — and as a person who may be known by persons — he chose three, before time began, to establish a relationship with his creatures. God the Father is Creator of all things, and the first principle of all the material laws which govern the reality known to humanity. He has benign intention towards his creatures, though the ultimate purpose of the creation remains unknown to them. The intensity of this intention finds its fulfilment, after the prolonged spiritual education of the Jewish people, in the person of the Son. Jesus is the Christ: he is God in the world, wholly God and wholly man, self-sent to procure human redemption, the King and Saviour. The preservation of believers in authentic knowledge of the Father and the Son is the office of the third person of the Trinity, the Holy Spirit. Where men and women are found in possession of truth the Holy Spirit is present, as the person who enables faith to have content and who allows it to have expression.

The doctrine of the Holy Trinity may be inferred or constructed from Scripture, but is not explicit in it. It is, however, the first-fruit of the Spirit at work in the Church — evident in the fullness of its depiction of God as soon as the Gospel of the Risen Christ came to be declared, and then revealed as the pre-existing nature of Godhead. In the operation of the Trinity, as practical fact in the earliest history of the Church, the words Jesus himself had used to describe the nature of God came to immediate fulfilment. In the Father, the Son of Man, and the Spirit, are three Persons who are One. It is no accident that the subtlety of the definition is typically Greek, for it was formulated by early believers who were immersed in the Hellenistic culture which existed among those who attended the first Councils of the Church. God is One and he is present among his people in the form of three persons: these persons are the same but are functionally different in relationship to humanity. The unitary God is also real — the Father made an actual creation, of matter and substance; the Son was not the appearance of a man but a man of the same flesh and blood as humanity; the Spirit is not like a pagan earth spirit or an ethereal impulse, but a person who visits the understanding of men and women and confers strengths beyond their own strengths. The Greek and Roman concept of 'personality' is important in this. It is a legal provision — a person who may inherit, and the three persons of the Holy Trinity not only constitute the creative energy of God, but are also in a sense the inheritors of the creation, forever involved with its destiny and never ceasing to be concerned with the individual fate of living things, even with the birds of the air (Matthew 6.26). From Jewish religious experience the Christian tradition inherited the concept of covenant. God has a relationship with his people which demands their response in a structured arrangement. At first conceived as the mere terms on which they would conquer territory for a homeland, in Christ the new covenant procured redemption for the whole of humanity, and transferred the terms from earthly rewards to the everlasting and celestial society of those who will ultimately see God. The Holy Spirit, again, may be seen at work as the person whose existence is detected by faithfulness to the covenant of Christ's great sacrifice, and can be experienced where human wilfulness is transcended by adhesion to the love of others.

The Holy Trinity is a mystery. The personal nature of God, as represented to men and women, is comprehensible; but the union of the three natures in one person is an assent of faith which, once made by the believer, confirms the true splendour of the creative love of God. The doctrine also enables the fallible senses of men and women to imagine God in more than a one-dimensional fashion, and this is a great advance on more primitive visions of divinity. Christians are called upon to have a relationship of prayer of obedience with each of the Three Persons, and to worship the unity of God of which they are the intimations.

THE CREATOR

Christians therefore affirm that God is not some 'First Cause' or 'Universal Spirit', but that he is a person. They also observe that the ancient misunderstandings about the nature of God recur through time, and are still to be looked for in present circumstances. Thus the notion of the Divine as some kind of energizing force has received renewed credence through the witness of science fiction, and the representation of God as a species of earth spirit, the error of pantheism, has abundant echoes among modern ecologists and enthusiasts for New Age religion. In Christianity, however, the personal nature of God may be known about because God has himself made men and women capable of discerning his true nature; he has endowed them with a sufficiency of his own attributes (they are made in his own image; Genesis 5.1) to enable them to enter into a relationship with him. In Christ the person of God became completely explicit; the universal became particular. The knowledge of God as person does not, of course, exhaust the full definition of the divine nature: there are presumably aspects, unconnected with the creation of the universe, and therefore unknowable by observation — and not revealed by divine intimation — to which humanity has no access. It is important in the Christian interpretation of God that the awesomeness of his supremacy enormously transcends understanding. The full nature of the divine, the purpose of the creation, and the nature of eternal existence outside of the cosmos remain mysteries. Precisely because God is a person who may be known by his creatures, it is possible for him to call them into a relationship — one in which the reason and reflective capacities imparted to humanity, but not to the rest of the animal creation, can be used to take part with God in the development of the planet and the consequent furtherance of the divine scheme. God is also properly addressed as a man, and not as a woman, because the cultures of the world have always regarded individual procreative initiative to be primarily a masculine attribute, suited, therefore, in symbolic description of the creation of the universe (and similar in kind to the depiction of the relationship of Christ to the Church as being like that of a bridegroom to his bride). The end and purpose of human life is most fully achieved when union with God is carried to the furthest extent of human capability. Yet, however intimate the individual relationship to God is there should never be, as it were, a familiarity with the divine: God remains august, removed, unknowable in the sum of his attributes, partially disclosed for reasons that are his and not ours, the supreme disposer of all things. He is owed fear and obedience as well as love. Humans may have established rights among themselves as a means of elevating social life and international association, but they have no rights in their relationship to God, whose sovereignty is absolute.

THE MISSION OF CHRIST

The entry of God into the world as a man, the Incarnation, confirmed the preceding anticipations of a purpose in the creation which humanity had discovered in the nature of the created order; it also advanced and completed the covenantal relationship which God had established with his people by both extending it to the whole of human society and by procuring a universal forgiveness for all those who entered the new covenant. The old covenant had established a relationship of law; the new offered a relationship of love. The grand implication — the divine strategy — of the Incarnation was the announcement that the primitive religious instincts of the human race had been correct in positing the existence and the works of God, and simultaneously, in the offering of himself made by Christ. The Incarnation brought about the redemption of men and women. In the former understanding of religion, the sins of the people were expiated through the sacrifice of animals; in the new, God gave himself, in an act of ultimate love and commitment, as the final great sacrifice, which secured forgiveness and the entry of those who confessed their sins to the life which was everlasting. The Kingdom proclaimed by Jesus begins in the lives of people while still living in the world — who are then joined to the unseen society of the blessed in eternity; to which, at death, those truly called by God are adhered. 'Predestination to Life is the everlasting purpose of God', as Article XVII of the Church of England declares, 'whereby (before the foundations of the world were laid) he hath constantly decreed by his counsel secret to us, to deliver from curse and damnation those whom he hath chosen in Christ out of mankind'.

Jesus shared the full attributes of a man, yet was without human sin. He was born naturally and was procreated directly by the divine use of the natural processes — yet without human agency in conception, and with the full sequence of human childbirth. Such conceptions by the gods were common enough in the sacred dramas of ancient paganism. In those religions however, congress between the gods, or between gods and mortals, was actual and corporeal: there is no suggestion of this in Christian understanding, and the birth of Jesus was to a pure Virgin, whose betrothed, St Joseph, acted as guardian and earthly father to the holy child. There are scriptural references to natural issue in the marriage of Joseph and Mary (Matthew 13.55) — James, the brother of the Lord, becoming head of the Church in Jerusalem after the death of Christ. For most of his life Jesus experienced conventional family association, thereby consecrating

11

earthly institutions and exemplifying God's desire to enter into a close relationship with his people. It was the mission of St John the Baptist which signalled the start of Jesus' own ministry, and his baptism by John prefigured the declaration of a universal new life.

It is important to notice, in view of the different priorities which each generation attributes to the message of Christ, that the biblical accounts of the ministry show him to be overwhelmingly concerned with the proclamation of a Kingdom. So much was this so, in fact, that Jews hearing his words at first assumed that he was fulfilling the messianic prediction of a restoration of the national autonomy of Israel. Yet the Kingdom of Christ was independent of time and circumstance and its citizenship, as soon became apparent, depended not on membership of a revived nation but on the forgiveness of sins. The message of Jesus was a call to repentance: the times were evil; the lives of people were given to them for explicit purposes (which excluded the pursuit of worldly comfort or mere considerations of welfare); the way of redemption was hard.

The works of mercy which Jesus performed — which he refused to make a sign of the Kingdom, but treated rather as concessions to human expectations of his divine claims — were not important or central in his ministry. The ethical ideals which he endorsed or adjusted were not very greatly at variance with the moral sense of his times: what mattered was his implicit authority to define ethical law — an indicator of his divine status. Ethical conduct, however, was inseparable from the life of the Kingdom, since it tested the seriousness of the convictions of individual believers and gave content, at the same time, to the collective community of those called to serve Christ, as he himself required, in the service of one another.

Thus far the life of Christ confirmed the old covenant. In the new messianic order, the redemption of humanity, it is not moral conduct but belief and submission which assume priority. The Kingdom is for sinners, and *all* are persistent in their sins. It is the mercy of God, in Christ, which elevates men and women and opens the gate of eternal life. A free gift is offered; eternal life cannot be earned by individual human effort, however sincerely made, or however moral the behaviour which is achieved. People are called to *believe* in Jesus, and to *trust* in God's providence — not in their own efforts. The priority of divine power over human achievement, of belief over action, was revealed in the decisive and mysterious events which indicated that Jesus was indeed God in the flesh. These were the Baptism, the Transfiguration, the Resurrection, and the Ascension: Christ identified by the Father and the Spirit, Christ mysteriously identified with the prophetic tradition, Christ truly and corporeally raised from the dead, Christ assumed bodily into the unseen world. Set within the context of these superlative and unprecedented sequences of divine authority was the Supper in the Upper Room, where he prepared for the perpetuation of his presence among his people in sacramental forms; the agony of Christ in Gethsemane, where he offered up his humanity in a prolonged prayer to the Father; and the great final expiation of sins in the Crucifixion. Then was the mission of God the Son completed. Now his work

continues through his body in the world —
the Church, the company of those who
believe in him. A perfect life has left an
example to an imperfect humanity; a perfect
sacrifice gives hope to sinners. The first man
to be received into Paradise, in the promise
of Christ himself, was a thief who was
crucified with him, and whose redemption
followed a simple expression of belief in
Jesus.

THE CREATION

All that we can know about reality derives
from experience of the physical created
order and our accumulated reflections about
it. Even those who have, throughout time,
believed themselves open to direct revelations of the Divine, in mystical transmissions
or in spiritual visitations, can only compre-
hend what they sense in the language and
symbolism supplied by the material world.
Christianity is in this sense a deeply material
religion: it regards the knowledge of God as
mediated through his creation, so that its
first intimations, and subsequent develop-

ments, will be rendered in accessible ways and interpreted in worldly images. Thus the centrality of the doctrine of the Incarnation — the universal Being of God, known about through human experience of the physical world, actually himself becomes a part of it in the person of a man, and so can be known as a person directly. Christianity is therefore also a human religion: it confirms the earliest intimations of the existence of God, however crudely these were rendered in primitive religion, and thus elevates the dignity of the human person — made to be a participant with God in the development of the planet — in the gift of forgiveness. Endowed with the capacities of reason and reflection, humans are called to understand their earthly context, and in doing so they will discover, not the full knowledge of God, but increasingly large amounts about the evidences of his creative power. It follows that the more that may be discovered about the nature of things, through scientific investigation and scholarly research, the more men and women can be admitted to an understanding of God's will. This may not always seem so at the time of discovery and analysis, for preceding cultural assumptions, the authority of earlier learning, or perhaps ambiguities in traditions of interpretations inherited from the past, may well inhibit ready acceptance. In order to protect humanity from too great a distortion, in this sense, God has made direct revelations of his nature and purposes, and entrusted them to certain traditions of human development, and it is these, the Church teaches, which can be known with certainty on the authority of Christ himself as mediated through his body in the world — the company of believers.

The material environment of humanity is unstable and finite. It is part of the vast clouds of dust and matter produced by some original explosion. This awesome creative power of God made the universe *ex nihilo*, out of nothing, and observation appears to suggest that the explosive force continues to impel the various fragments of matter, including the solar system and the earth, to unimaginable distances. In the beginning, as the Book of Genesis declares, 'the earth was a formless void' (Genesis 1.2). There are also allusive echoes in Scripture to darkened skies and ancient cataclysms, when the sun was obscured and people suffered terrible privations — suggestions, perhaps, of terrestrial experience of collisions with other pieces of space debris, whose memory, from the very earliest times, seems to have resonated in folk-myth. The earth, the vehicle of human life, is thus most likely to be a temporary sphere of dust, caught, as it were, in extreme slow motion, somewhere between creation and extinction. This is actually an important dimension of the religious understanding of the world, for the Judaic-Christian tradition has always accounted the world to be a temporary phenomenon, moving inexorably towards final great disaster — expressed, probably not inaccurately, in terms of fire. Unlike the interpretation of some other religious traditions, the Church has persistently declined to represent the earth as in a kind of eternal recurrence of cyclical being, or as locked into the predictable sequences of a determined programme. The earth has been seen as a hazardous place, full of suffering for the creatures who sustain a precarious existence amongst all the living matter which coats its surface. In the beginning, creation; at the end, judgement: between the two the planet hurtles towards inevitable destruction. With limited information, and carrying around substantial amounts of erroneous data from preceding generations, the Church has at times embraced mistaken interpretations of the courses of the planetary spheres. This is of no consequence. What matters is the astonishing majesty of the creation, the power of the Creator, the finite nature of all things: in such matters the Church has always been realistic, and its witness to the truly decisive importance of matter itself has been unswerving. Humans are creatures, inseparable in their sensations and identities, and in their material condition and prospects, from all other components of the creation. You are dust, God told them, and to dust you will return (Genesis 3.19). The biblical account is again accurate: God made the world first, and it was good for his purpose — which we cannot know. Then he made men and women, and put them into an environment which does not provide the personal security and freedom from pain which they came, with increasing insistence, to demand, and which forms the basis of their alienation. And there is the everlasting frustration of men and women, and the unending wrongness of their priorities. God made the world for his purposes, not for ours. The rebellion of humanity, the first primordial disobedience, the descent into Original Sin, derived from humanity's very pursuit of a worldly security which is contrary to the nature of creation. It was thus a rebellion against the will of God.

NATURAL AND REVEALED TRUTH

Knowledge of God derives both from observation of the natural order, the creation, and from special revelations made about himself by God. The first provides the basis of Natural, and the second of Revealed Religion.

The perception of the Divine has been available to all peoples from the beginning, and seems to have been inseparable from the self-consciousness of human identity which occurred gradually in the lengthy translation of the species from the simpler life-forms of the primordial swamp to civilized society. Sometimes these impressions of the existence of God have been rooted in ordinary human need, when 'God' is envisaged as a provider of harvest and an assistance in daily toil; sometimes, in more elevated moments, as an explanation of order in the existence of things; sometimes as an extension of human self-esteem; sometimes as the awesome mover of cosmic events. Such intimations of the Divine produce varying projections of the presence of God: as a spirit inherent in natural objects; as a life-force or animating cause; as the inhabitant of inaccessible places like mountain tops or subterranean caverns; as the shade of the dead; as a supreme person. The religious ideas of the peoples of the world reflect or embody aspects of these insights, some of which have origins and purposes which consigned them to perpetual degeneracy, and some of which prompted truly important developments in the idea of God. The major religions of the world, unlike the pervasive animism from which they are a development, are valued precisely because their foundations were laid in the real presence of

God in his creation. But they remain latencies: the God who is known about through observation of the natural order is descriptive rather than authentically active, and reflects the consciousness of humanity in static moments of past development rather than in the dynamic of unfolding and progressive essays in truth. There is much that is noble and real in the great world religions, and the Judaic-Christian dispensation shares some features in common with them; they are not, however, in the Christian view, complete understandings of God, being, in effect, versions of aspects of his nature, recounted in a manner which excludes the superlative sacred drama of forgiveness and redemption which lies at the heart of the Christian account of God's mercy. Natural Religion has the additional disadvantage of tending to revert to pre-occupation with the very world of nature which prompted its origins, and therefore periodically to produce latter-day projections of human need as the basis of faith. Yet for all that, the knowledge of God derived from observation of the natural order remains important in Christianity, for relationships in human society are largely conditioned by features of the natural world, both the primary environment of the physical planet and the secondary environment of social and intellectual reflexion — and the regulation of such relationships describes the world of morality. The raw material of human ethical consciousness thus remains the experience of the world itself. It is not possible to have a moral relationship between people and God, since God is a sovereign without limitation, and people are creatures without rights. The relationship between humanity and the Divine is a relationship of unconditional obedience. Between individual human creatures, however, and within human social or national collectives, there are of course relationships which are moral. Morality exists as the reverse of arbitrary conditions in social relationships; it may be said to be in effect when conduct is calculated according to known rules of behaviour. All the world religions, reflecting the needs of the natural order, contain moral ideas, and the higher religions enshrine ethical systems. But they accompany the primary religious insight, which relates to the obligations owed to the Creator, and in some senses emanate from it; they are not in themselves more than that, however. It has been a heresy in many religions to elevate mere morality above the first demands of the sovereignty of God — a condition which inevitably accords priority to human needs and welfare and gives emphasis to human capabilities for self-improvement over the supreme power of God. Yet morality is crucially important; it not only provides for the existence of society, it also provides the content of the obedience owed to God in the real conditions of social exchange. Part of the revelation made by God, in Judaic-Christian understanding, also included moral injunctions laid down by God for his creatures, so furnishing the conditions on earth in which the flowers of spirituality could grow and flourish. Morality, then, belongs essentially to Natural Religion but needs completion in revealed truth; Revelation itself provides doctrinal statements about the nature of God.

Modern people find difficulties with the details of revealed truths precisely because they are so specific. Ours is an intellectual culture which prefers the general to the particular when it comes to religious ideas. But God began to make himself known to humans at a time in their development — as social evolution allowed it — when it was the small and detailed context which impressed. As in the philosophical speculations of the Greek Sophists, the universal, in order to be known about, needs explicit particularization in the world of human understanding. Ultimately, in the Incarnation of Christ, God himself becomes known about by becoming himself a man: the perfect and most complete example of the particularization of the universal. First, God had made himself known to a particular people. Among those sensitive to the discoveries of Natural Religion the Jewish people had the most articulated sense of the supreme insight that God is a unitary Being. They envisaged other peoples with other gods; but the God of the Jews — first envisaged crudely as a divinity of mountain and fire, a salvation god who leads his quasi-nomadic people through adverse circumstances to eventual nationhood — came to be seen as possessed of universal attributes and to be, in himself, one. His self-revelation is described in the Bible which the Jews taught and venerated, known to us as the Old Testament. It was progressive. To the moral law (The Ten Commandments), vouchsafed to Moses, a covenant was adhered. This followed the style of treaties made between peoples at that time: it laid out obligations owed to God in return for certain blessings attached to independent nationhood, and added a tariff of penalties should the terms of the covenant be violated. In itself, and in human terms, there was nothing especially remarkable about the relationship of the Jews and the Creator, and it was paralleled in other examples in the ancient world. Here was God, building a knowledge of himself within the expectations of a given people, derived from their perception of Natural Religion. What *was* remarkable, however, was the religious genius of the Jewish people which from then on developed the further succession of revelations made by God: through historical events, through prophetic discernment, through insights into the natures of men and women themselves. And, finally, in Christ, the one who came as the Saviour, not of the small national aspirations which their religious tradition had appeared to indicate, but of the world.

Revealed truth is primarily about doctrine. It is about the nature of God himself. Even when it is given in the form of moral injunction or exhortation the content of the message and the authority exercised in its transmission is about the nature of God: that he is a person, that he is involved with his creatures and their destiny, that he is sovereign, that he is represented in the world in a triune form (Father, Son, and Holy Spirit) which existed from the beginning, that he has a relationship with humanity which demands a response, that he has ordered the salvation of the world. Revealed truth was made, and is being made to this day, both individually, to those open to prophetic understanding — but whose understanding nevertheless needs to be tested against the collective deposit of the faith of the whole People of God — and collectively to all those who stand in the tradition of believers and who exist, in time and in eternity, as the Church of Christ. It is a matter of debate as to whether the revelation made to the first Christians was static, or whether, over time, it 'develops', so that new doctrines unfold, as it were teleologically, as the branches of a plant expand (Mark 4.31). Protestants have tended to the first view; those in the Catholic tradition, from St Vincent of Lérins to Newman, have argued the second. Definitions of dogma made in recent centuries in the Catholic Church (Papal Infallibility, the Immaculate Conception, the Assumption of the Virgin), indicate the vitality of the idea within the largest of the Christian Churches. The Church of England has no means of defining a position in relation to the dynamics of doctrinal development, but plainly veers to the Protestant position which prevailed among the Reformers whose voices were most decisive at the time when its formularies were drawn up in the sixteenth century.

Revealed truth is to be recognized as an advance on Natural Religion, a stage reached in the past of humanity, when the more basic needs of primitive society were superseded by sophisticated concepts of the divine mind. God was still envisaged, however, as being like a glorified earthly ruler and his court, and the symbolical language used about God, derived from such processes, persists to this day. It is in some sense unavoidable. God cannot be imagined in abstract. Earthly rulers in our own age are not a good model: they are either democratic ciphers or frank tyrants, and God is neither. This, however, mostly poses a problem for the other world religions. Christianity does not need an earthly exemplar of the authority of God, for it has, at the centre of its Revealed truth, an actual man: the man who was God — Christ. Christians do not have to imagine or construct an image of the Divine Being because in Jesus they can see the fullness of Revealed truth. When Christ came into the world the world was itself irradiated with the divine essence, which remains to the end of time. If you would see God look at Christ. Then religion became no longer latent or descriptive; it became, in the mission of Jesus, active. He came not only to confirm that the preceding intimations of the existence of God were properly, if crudely, stated, but that God's activity in the world was extended to salvation. The great act of expiation for human sin produced the issue of the divine dispensation: the paradox of the Crucifixion, which was the harbinger of eternal life for those whose sins caused it; the great love of God was the essential revelation made to a race who were definitely unworthy of it. Revealed truth, in its finest and most decisive expression, delivers to men and women the priceless and complete gift of forgiveness.

HUMAN LIFE

From among the teeming mass of living things which cover the surface of the earth God has called men and women to occupy a special relationship with him, and he has, accordingly, endowed them with the capacities of reason and reflection. In this, they are unlike the rest of the animal creation, and unlike also the smallest units of living matter from which all living things are constituted, and are progressively admitted, through their own discoveries about the nature of reality, to a dynamic role in the furtherance of the divine scheme. Their highest characteristic is their potential for immortality. Yet they remain inseparable from the rest of the creation, and are subject to the same laws of matter as direct the destinies of all things. Men and women can themselves, as beings with reason and a sense of self-worth, imagine more ideal circumstances for life: this is an early token of their propensity to rebel against the order in which God has placed them, and in every age produces human dissatisfaction. Although creative in one sense, in that human discontent spurs advance and discovery, in many ways this assists an alienation of humanity from God: people seek accommodations with their own desire for security and ultimate knowledge which are incompatible with their status as creatures. They are also liable to romanticize other animal life-forms, and to endow them in imagination with human emotional responses, in a way which unrealistically assesses the true separation of humanity from the rest of the creation. Men and women alone have the capacity for immortality, and the rest of created life exists to witness to universal purposes of God which are not disclosed to human judgement.

Neither the divine providence for men and women, nor their use of the gift of intelligence, however, exempts them from their material nature. They are made of the substance of the planet and are conditioned by it. There is nothing mysterious in the constitution of humans; God has willed an arrangement of things whereby knowledge and experience is directly related to circumstance. The earth itself provides information about the nature of people as creatures inseparable from the same material conditions that direct the destinies of all things: the human image of God, whether devised through natural sources or through the presence of God in Christ, derives from the conditioning of the physical planet and the collected wisdom of those who inhabit its surface. What is called the *soul* is the individual identity of each person evaluated as a candidate for eternity — it is not, as in some ancient heresies, a kind of mysterious spark or internal heavenly presence. What is called *conscience* is not the agent of external spiritual sense, but simply collected memory of accumulated moral teaching. Hence the supreme importance which Christians attach to the formation of conscience — to extensive and precise moral instruction of the young. Nurture of the soul, correspondingly, through early introduction to spiritual exercises and a continued education in spirituality throughout life, is an essential condition in the formation of the spiritual person.

Unlike the optimism about human nature which describes so much modern speculation about the capacities for good or evil inherent in men and women, Christians have always regarded the prevalence of human corruption as being the leading characteristic of the human condition. In the Christian view of the world, men and women are not liable to evil because of deficiencies in their social conditioning or their absorption of wrong ideologies, but because they are human. There is something disjointed at the centre of each person which is out of all proportion to their ability for self-correction. They are less, that is to say, than the agents required for God's original plan. Somewhere in the remote past the alienation between God and humankind interrupted primordial innocence; there was a stage at which the invitation to men and women to co-operate with God in the progressive development of life on earth was abused by them to the extent that — in the language of biblical imagery — there was a 'Fall'. Gifts of reason and reflection imparted for purposes defined by the divine will were then diverted to satisfying human claims to a measure of autonomy. People became self-consciously possessed of ambitions which were not part of the providential vision: it was this 'Original Sin' which came to determine the nature of all people, and is inherent in everyone, so that even their highest aspirations are somehow alloyed to baser instincts. The result is the extraordinary dilemma of humanity — a race capable of the highest thoughts and of assembling the most sublime images of perfection, yet one which is actually burdened, through the horrific facts of human nature, with the permanence of corruption. The genius of the Christian religion, and therefore of the message of Christ himself, is that those who regret their sins, and the terrible evidences of their fallen nature, are freely admitted by God to complete forgiveness. Men and women who adhere to the promises of Christ remain corrupted in their natures, but are redeemed and then achieve status as creatures in transition to blessedness.

MODERN HUMANISM

With the decline of Christianity in developed societies there has come an elevation of humanity. It is men and women and their welfare who now preoccupy not only moral inclinations — which to some extent they always did — but the area once devoted to spirituality. Indeed the concept of 'spirituality' itself has been secularized, and is now increasingly used to describe any human attitudes or instincts which dignify people or allow them aesthetic or moral reflection. The perspective of eternity has been redirected to the earth; spirituality, as a concept, has been robbed of authentic transcendence. The aspirations of men and women have become sovereign, and are circumscribed, not by obedience owed to the laws of God, but by considerations related to welfare or the duties of citizenship. This 'deification' of humanity is subtle and persuasive. Christians themselves often identify the central tenets of their own faith — redefined in terms of its ethical content — as embodiments of the same love of neighbour. And there are in fact similarities. Christians certainly have the obligation to give real expression to the love of Christ by attending to the needs of others and thereby serving Christ himself. But secular humanism raises human need to a position which excludes the ideological purposes of life, which Christians have always regarded as the priority. What a person believes is more important than his material condition or welfare: this bare statement of Christian essentials is unacceptable to modern humanism, which urges welfare above doctrine. In reality, of course, humanists are self-deceived, and beneath the various programmes of social alleviation they are actually propagating ideological beliefs derived from basic materialism as a world picture. Christians are liable to overlook, or fail to notice, the philosophical materialism implicit in the welfare priority, and to acclaim it — not as their own replacement, which it is — as an expression of applied Christianity. Yet the love of God precedes the love of neighbour, and the culture of rights and entitlements which now accompanies welfare materialism reduces its potential to be an acceptable adjunct of true Christian service. The present elevation of humanity is not an exemplification of Christianity but the identification of its probable successor.

Some believe that there is a space in the human psyche which religion fills. To the extent that this may be true there is nothing mysterious in the phenomenon; it is cultural. People have been socially conditioned to self-regard, and the pursuit of individual meaning and significance (which *is* related to the divine endowments of reason and reflection) appears capable of assuming virtually any cultural arrangement. Modern substitutes for religion are easily recognizable and are patently gathering their adherents. All are indications of human vanity or the desire for welfare. Moral authoritarianism also appears to be as pervasive as ever, even in a society which prides itself on its liberalism. It, too, has been secularized and serves welfare ends.

BLASPHEMY

Blasphemy exists where humans attempt to substitute for God, interposing their desires or ideal schemes in place of the divine will. Lesser expressions of blasphemy, but still serious in point of gravity, subsist in explicit rejections of the holiness of God — lesser, however, because these are likely to be inspired by transient passions, and so do not represent sustained or considered philosophical commitment.

THE EFFICACY OF GOD'S WORKS

Just as the knowledge of God's action in the world is acquired through human experience of the natural order, and the interpretation of revealed truth is conditioned by images and language derived from the natural order, so God's action in relation to his creatures is effected through the laws of matter and causation which he has established. He does not work, so to say, by magic. Yet men and women persistently expect a magical or miraculous element to operate in the world of religious understanding, and to suppose, indeed, that their own sense of religious experience will have a dimension which is incapable of material explanation. Hence the widespread confusion between aesthetic sensation and authentic spirituality; it rests on the conviction that religious teaching is not objectively true but depends upon the operation in the individual of some kind of special 'uplifting' faculty. People, however, may be moved in this manner by all kinds of worldly contrivances of the emotions — some of which may usefully give fine tune to understandings of God, or provide proper ways of offering up to God, in worship, the noblest that can be imagined by men and women in worldly accomplishments such as music or art. Religious and secular ideologies of all sorts (and some of the basest kind), have as a matter of recent record been celebrated and propagated by the use of exactly the same varieties of cultural sensation as have adorned religious feeling. Humans are very easily manipulated, especially when the appeal is directly to the emotions. The work of God is accomplished through the mediation of the creation he has set in order, and Christianity is in this sense an historical religion. It is affected by the conditions of change in which it is set and may in turn, as in the last two millennia, affect the world around it. The Church collectively interprets God's will over time, and the message conveyed is perpetually being reinterpreted as the world changes. Yet it is, in essentials, always the same; for to be true to the dynamic of the divine scheme the operations of God have to be seen to be progressive. This is equally true in the vocation of the individual believer. All life is change, as Newman observed, and to be perfect is to have changed often. Time unfolds things both new and old, and the prophetic role of all believers in all circumstances is to learn the signs of the time, and to read eternal messages in the transience and flux of the passing order. There is nothing mysterious about this. Christian truth is derived from the common data available to all who seek meaning: its exclusivity and unique authority come from the divine intervention made once for all in the person of Christ.

There is, therefore, a miraculous core in the Christian understanding of the world, but it is properly recognized in exceptional effusions of divine grace, in special revelations of the divine Person, rather than in the mechanics of daily events. As a general rule it may be calculated that operations which involve direct revelations of God's authority are exceptional events. The creation of the universe itself is such a direct and therefore miraculous event, since it occurred out of nothing, though in the act of taking place it set up laws which subsequently governed the formation and dispersal of matter. There are examples of miraculous interventions in the Old Testament: the confirmation of the laws given to Moses being one such. But the supreme example is the Incarnation of Christ, with all its consequent circumstances. There is, perhaps, in the accounts of the earthly ministry of Jesus, a mixture of interpretation, in which the truth being taught becomes expressed in the images of a folk miracle — the wedding at Cana, for example. Though the truth being conveyed is important the miraculous element which may have been added in pious meaning, or in accordance with popular preaching styles at the time, is not. This is plainly of a different category of importance from the fact of the Incarnation or the Resurrection or the Ascension, where the same creative and miraculous power deployed by God in the origin of all things is witnessed again through the birth, death, and departure of God himself in the full materiality of the life he shared with men and women. Christians cannot interpret these events symbolically: the words of Christ and the testimony of the centuries identify them as miraculous.

The promise of Christ to his followers that they would perform work comparable to his own (Luke 10.9), and St Paul's ministry among the earliest Christians, make it clear that a miraculous dimension is still resident among the People of God. The Church, however, has always very properly regarded 'ecclesiastical miracles' with some reserve. Humanity has a ready capacity for self-deception, and is, in relation to acceptance of knowledge of all varieties, only too ready to believe what it wants to believe. Although the ways of God are not our ways, and his will is discerned in events which surprise us, there is a reasonable probability that for an allegedly miraculous occurrence to be considered authentic it must in some sense amplify or glorify the knowledge of God. It is difficult to see otherwise why a divinity who so overwhelmingly operates through the real material world should suspend his own laws in order to correct minor human afflictions. Miraculous healing, which formed a part in Christ's revelation of his majesty, does not in general tend to reveal much that is consonant with religious phenomenology as understood by Christian believers. These healings are anyway often trivial and marginal, and seemingly affect only certain kinds of affliction. God's healing powers are better understood as mediated by those who have attempted to share in his purposes by seeking to develop the world. Medicine has always formed a part of the Christian ministry, and it has eschewed magic in order to advance science.

THE SACRAMENTS

The Incarnation was the supreme use of the materiality of the creation to further the divine scheme of redemption, but there are other special rites, instituted by Christ, in which the truths of God receive earthly expression. Of these the Church of England recognizes Baptism and the Holy Eucharist as authentic sacraments necessary for individual participation in the scheme of salvation. The important fact about the sacraments is that they are objectively true: they do not depend upon the human senses or human responses to have real effect, and the unworthiness of those who perform the rites in which they are delivered, or of those who receive them, does not in any way detract from their sacred character. When the Church performs the ceremonies associated with the sacramental function, for example, there may be accompanying transports of fellowship or a sense of Christian communal identity; these, however, are not of the essence of the sacrament, but are external accidents. The sacraments are true in themselves. Despite some difficulties of precise definition, which believers through the centuries have encountered, the objective reality of sacramental grace — the operation of the Holy Spirit in the act of Baptism, and the real presence of the Lord in the Holy Communion — are present without any reference to the human condition of those involved in the rites. Grace is the means by which God sanctifies his people, and grace is received independently of human understanding, in the promise which he has made to present his benefits under the earthly forms available to his creatures.

Jesus himself gave his direct authority to the rite of Baptism by himself receiving the Baptism of John. The symbolism of water in cleansing from sin has universal expression in different cultures, and this providentially offers an entry into the Christian life which is easily accessible to the senses of all people. In Christian Baptism all sins are forgiven, both Original Sin, and the ordinary sins of omission and commission which derive from concupiscence (the inherent liability to sin which all people have as part of their status as created beings). Although forgiven, however, the nature of men and women (or children) remains unchanged, and so therefore does the effect of Original Sin in producing personal corruption, and the fruits of concupiscence in prompting actual sins in daily lives. Christian believers receive the promise of forgiveness, but their liability to sin is not diminished — except in the ordinary human sense that those who attempt to lead a disciplined and ideologically structured life may achieve a measure of success in avoiding some occasions of sin (a phenomenon encountered in secular as in religious experience). Because Baptism is objectively effective it can be received by infants. Indeed, human societies naturally wish to nurture their young in principles of truth, and do not hesitate to indoctrinate them from the earliest age in the current sacral values of the society (race equality, for example, or democratic polity). Since Christians believe in the objective benefits of the life of grace imparted by Baptism it would not be desirable to withhold them from people of the youngest age, and infant Baptism has always been the practice of the Church. It requires, however, on the assurance of godparents or other sponsors, that the child so initiated shall be taught the principles of Christian truth and be eventually brought to confirmation in them. Baptism is entry into the Church of Christ; it is absolutely essential for all those who are to take their place in constituting the body of Christ in the world and in becoming inheritors of the Kingdom of Heaven. It is the means of entering into the priesthood of all believers. There is also an ancient tradition of acceptance that those who were to be dedicated by their parents to Christian upbringing, but who die early or who were converted later in life and die without the opportunity of receiving baptismal rites, are nevertheless baptized by their death into the eternal life of Christ.

The sacrament of the Lord's Supper constitutes the central act of Christian worship, and follows the instruction of Jesus himself that his last meal with his disciples should be perpetuated. It is not an occasion of mere fellowship, however, but the presence of Christ himself. To those who 'rightly, worthily, and with faith' receive this sacrament, according to the formularies of the Church of England, the bread 'is a partaking of the Body of Christ; and likewise the Cup of Blessing is a partaking of the Blood of Christ' (Article XXVIII). The Church of England denies that there is any material change in the sacred elements used in the rite (transubstantiation), but upholds the ancient belief that the presence of Christ in the Holy Eucharist transcends the evidences of the senses. Whereas the rite plainly has some of the characteristics of a memorializing or commemorative event it is also taken to impart a special grace of Christ — his very body and blood, truly received in faith. It was believed in the early Church that angels gathered round the altar when the priest offered the sacred words of institution — an indication of the effect of the sacrament in uniting the seen and the unseen worlds, and in reminding the People of God that they exist simultaneously both in time and in eternity. The presence of the unseen community of those who love God is inseparable from the objective truth of the sacrament: Christ really is here, and so is the witness of the hosts of believers who are now in eternity. The Blessed Sacrament of the altar is to be especially venerated and to be affirmed with the greatest reverence available to humankind, because it is the Last Supper itself, and no mere representation, which occurs when the people gather around the holy table. It is Christ who presides at the altar: his sacred action, forever performed for humanity, expressed through the officiating minister. The forgiveness of sins through the enactment of the new covenant, the great expiation in the death of the Saviour himself, is a present reality, an intimation of the blessedness of eternity, and an exercise for those still in the world of the dignity of celestial citizenship. The Lord's Supper is the gateway to the Kingdom of Heaven, the place where time exchanges with the mystery of the eternal. It is not necessary to understand the exact means by which grace is transmitted for even the most humble intellect to receive the fullness of God's mercy.

THE AUTHORITY OF SCRIPTURE

During his earthly ministry the Lord delivered his truth not to a set of writings but to a living group of witnesses — who after his death became his body in the world, the Church. It was from these people that the record of Christ's message, with appended evidences of his continuing work among his people, derived: the New Testament. The account of God's progressive education of his people, and the Bible known to Christ, already existed as the Old Testament. The two sets of sacred writings together comprise the canon of Christian Scripture; they bear the authority of those who identified their authenticity as a true record, who rejected unsatisfactory alternative books, and who undertook to regard them as containing information necessary for salvation (Article VI). It was therefore the Church itself which produced the Scriptures — which, in consequence, may be said to reflect the presence of Christ amongst his earliest followers and so to contain his authority. However inspirational the writing, these books are nevertheless the work of human minds; those who wrote or transmitted amended versions of them were doubtless enveloped in spiritual discipline but they were still men. Numerous passing phases of culture are reflected in the books of the Old Testament — nomadic, tribal, nationalist; the experience of kingship and the experience of exile, of conquest and of being conquered. These records may be compared with contemporaneous records of the vicissitudes of other ancient peoples: God chose the Jewish people for the most perfect education in a knowledge of his creative purposes, but he also disclosed evidences of himself through the pre-history and history of other peoples. The New Testament is not a complete account of the life of Christ and nor is it a chronicle of the early Church. It was written not to describe the Christian religion but to prove it. It can contain no internal evidence which may be used to discredit any part of its account of Christ for it was precisely put together as a narrative of proofs that he was the Messiah. It is an account of faith and not of history, though cast in the form of a sequence of events.

All the books of the Bible employ a language of imagery and symbolism which reflects the assumptions and commonplaces of a culture which has passed away. It is not as alien to modern understanding as might seem otherwise, probably because the Bible, as part of Western heritage, has itself perpetuated some of these understandings of the world and given them an intellectual currency which still exists. This consideration introduces further subtleties into modern use of the Bible, and the crucial work of separating those things which related to a dead culture from those which convey the core message remains fraught with difficulty. Hence the vocation of biblical scholarship for which the Church has always made careful provision. There is some danger at the present time that this vocation will itself become secularized, should the *magisterium* (or teaching office of the Church) fail to make adequate provision for dedicated Christian scholarship in institutions or courses conducted under its exclusive auspices. The intellectual methods used in biblical enquiry are exactly the same as those used in all knowledge; the sacred text is necessarily subjected to the same tests as every source of information should be. But biblical scholarship is different from secular enquiry because the truth which the Bible relates is already known to be true through the witness of the living body of the believers — the Church itself. The intention, therefore, is not to determine truth but to unfold the manner in which it has been delivered: a prophetic work whose result will be a continuing enrichment of Christian understanding. The Bible was not written for intellectuals but for those who receive the faith, in the words of Christ himself, as little children might do (Luke 18.17). Although a knowledge of the social and religious context in which Christianity had its origins may be useful in avoiding some mistakes of interpretation it should not lead to radical reassessment for one clear reason. The religion of Jesus is not a resuscitation of past beliefs but the fruit of a continuing tradition of belief. What is called Christianity is what Christian believers have determined that it is through centuries of reinterpretation and reapplication; it is organic and dynamic, and the authority of the Scriptures provides pointers to ways in which the forever changing body of Christian ideas should relate to the message once delivered to the tradition in which Christ stood and which his living body transmits. The Bible is to be reverenced as the repository of the record of God's dealings with humanity; the human means by which the will of God was written down were not transformed in the process, however, and the truths of the Bible are not often self-evident. They require interpretation, and as matter of historical fact they have been variously interpreted in different moments of Christian development. The authority to recognize a legitimate interpretation from a partial or corrupt one lies with the whole body of Christ's people, the Church, acting collectively.

THE CREEDS

Three abbreviated statements of faith (or creeds) are recognized by the Church of England — the Apostles' Creed, the Nicene Creed, and the Creed of St Athanasius. All three have been sanctioned by early Councils of the Church. They are incorporated into liturgical use so that adherents may make a profession of faith in the context of worship. The doctrines enunciated in the creeds are to be believed wholly. (The Church of England thus requires belief in the 'Double Procession of the Holy Spirit', the *filioque* clause which defines the Spirit as proceeding from the Father *and* the Son. This follows the decree of the Council of Chalcedon in 451, and differs from the historic custom of the Orthodox Churches, although it is agreeable to the use of Latin Christianity. The definition of the Double Procession does not impair the equality of the Spirit with the Father and the Son, since all three Persons of the Holy Trinity are from eternity and existed before the world was made.)

THE BLESSED VIRGIN MARY

Christian tradition has always given a special place of honour to the Virgin as the person — selected out of all humanity — who brought the Son of God into the world. It was at the Council of Ephesus (431) that Mary was recognized with the title of *Theotokos*, or 'Mother of God'. The relationship of the Church of England to the cult of

the Virgin is unclear, however. The definitions of the Immaculate Conception and the
Assumption, though believed in by Christians since the earliest times, were only
formally acclaimed as doctrines by the
Roman Catholic Church in the last century
and a half. They have always been part of
Orthodox teaching. Despite a traditional
rhetoric of opposition to Mariolatry from
within the Anglican leadership, following
Protestant use, and the decline of popular
devotions to the Virgin in the years after the
English Reformation, the Church of England
has never formally taken a position on the
exact nature of the honour due to Mary, nor
on her place in the scheme of salvation. Yet
a position may be inferred from the
sustained disinclination of the leadership,
over the centuries, to encourage spiritual
exercises in which the Virgin is mediator;
she has received none of the titles of honour
for liturgical recognition which are a familiar
characteristic of the historic Churches.
Respected theological writers, in the nine-
teenth century in particular, have explicitly
argued against the cult of the Virgin,
especially as then understood in the ultra-

montane devotional practices of Roman Catholicism. It is possible, but not realistic, to contend that the Church of England is, by negative deduction, not hostile to Marian devotions on the grounds that there have been no authoritative retractions of those decrees of the early Councils of the universal Church which originally sanctioned them. But the Church of England does not have the constitutional means of making any such pronouncements, so the matter remains indecisively open, and attitudes to the place of the Virgin differ according to styles of churchmanship and spiritual psychology. There can be no doubt — for it is a matter of historical record — that the Church of England has in practice conducted its liturgical development and its theological exegesis as if the Virgin has no place in the scheme of salvation beyond that of being the human mother of the Lord. Paradoxically, however, the modern Church has decided, in its liturgical calendar, to choose the day in August which is universally recognized as the Feast of the Assumption as a special feast of Mary. It is surely disingenuous to suppose that the selection of this day was

unassociated with the doctrine of the
Assumption or that Marian devotions would
not thereby be encouraged. Perhaps the
question is best regarded as one in which
Anglican opinion is in transition.

JUDGEMENT

A substantial part of the teaching of Christ
related directly to a coming judgement,
when men and women would be accountable
to God for the use they have made of the gift
of life. Modern people, however, find the
fact of judgement extremely hard to believe,
preferring, instead, a kind of unstructured
universalism in which God's ultimate clem-
ency extends to every person regardless of
belief and action. It is likely that this notion
derives from human vanity and a disinclination to recognize the gravity of personal sin
or the seriousness with which individual
culpability is to be taken. The sayings of
Jesus (John 5.27–30, the separation of the
wheat and the tares, for example, or, more
famously, the sheep and the goats) persistently return to a judgement in which there

will be a decisive act of divine discrimination. Doubtless the symbolism attached to the place where those will go who are excluded from the company of the blessed is unhelpful to modern understanding; the images reflect cosmic models of reality which are no longer credible. But the substance of the teaching is unaltered: God will judge each life, and those who have used their time on earth to anticipate the values of eternity will be called to the service of God and to blessedness. Eternal life begins in material life: that part of each person which incorporates aspects of the life of the Kingdom of Christ has, in life, already begun to fashion the spiritual body which emerges from death. Those who have not assembled a spiritual life on earth will find that there is nothing to survive death except the weight of their sins. No person should ever forget, none the less, that the irreproachable mercy of God extends to all who in life confess their sins, try to amend their lives, and seek to educate themselves in a knowledge of God's will. This last point is important and is often neglected in modern society. Religious truth is not self-explanatory, and spiritual formation requires the person to acquire information about the nature of God. Christians, furthermore, believe that no one comes to the Father except through the dispensation of Christ (John 14.6), and that however noble and helpful other religious traditions may be in the insights they offer, it is the death of Jesus which alone activates redemption. Before Christ came into the world those who sought out the service of God in their lives, and endured numerous privations and even death in the process — 'of whom the world was not worthy' (Hebrews 11.38) — nevertheless received the promise of Christ and were blessed accordingly. They are recognized as saints of the Church. But Christ has fulfilled their expectations, and those living today are required to serve God by standing in the tradition of belief which he established, and to accept the cup of blessing which he blessed. Christian truth is often rendered in its own interpretive images and symbols, and it describes realities which are frequently unlike the expectations of the modern world. The language of spirituality is, accordingly, not just picked up from the surrounding culture — it needs to be learned. It also needs to be applied, and it is in the application (the love of neighbour) that its deepest meanings are sometimes disclosed. The work of Christian education, both in personal spiritual formation, and in providing institutions in which a knowledge of the faith can be transmitted, is as important today as it has ever been. So is the obligation, in Christian parents, to teach the faith to their children. The supposition, often heard today, that young people can 'make up their own minds' about religion when they reach years of maturity is not sustainable. The secular world does not leave them in a moral vacuum when it comes to socializing children and instructing them in the virtues of modern humanism — because those secular dogmas are believed to be self-evidently true. If subscription to, for example, democratic practice or racial equality, is made obligatory in our culture, as it is, doubtless for good reason, then Christians who believe in their faith should certainly instruct their children in it from the earliest age. They will, in the process, be fulfilling the vows made in Baptism.

Judgement, then, relates to the content of individual lives. Those lives, to be in accordance with the mind of Christ, need a daily infusion of the knowledge of God. When men and women attempt their own spiritual education, and recognize their need for a strength which exceeds their own strength, and admit the frailty of their best endeavours, and rely on the providence of God to bring their subdued understanding into correspondence with the splendours of Christian truth, then the Holy Spirit may confidently be said to be in operation. No person is ever alone who seeks to take the steps of spiritual formation: for such a person is then already in the company of the blessed, and has already begun the construction of an eternal home in the ambiguous circumstances of daily life. This education, however, is not to be attempted without guidance from the spiritual tradition inherited from the *magisterium*, or teaching office, of the Church. Whether it is in understanding the meaning of the sacred text of Scripture, or in constructing an application of moral law, Christians are part of an organic body of believers, and their judgement must derive from the collective wisdom of the centuries — as reflected in the formal teachings of religious authority. The modern tendency to theological and ecclesiological eclecticism, to make up religious truth by self-selection, is anathema to Christian understanding and inevitably results in the gravest errors. The Church is no other than the body of Christ in the world, and it is *his* teaching which it guards and has an obligation to propagate, not the opinions of individuals.

At the time of Christ the question of the resurrection of the dead was a matter of great controversy, one of a number which divided the Pharisees and the Sadducees, and which both inside Judaism and in the various practices of the Greek world had given rise to a large number of resurrection cults. Jesus was decisively clear that the resurrection of the dead is a reality, and in his own glorious Resurrection he redeemed the material nature of humanity by a resuscitation of the actual body. When the creed speaks of 'the resurrection of the body' of believers, however, it refers to the survival, after death, of the whole nature of the individual spiritual personality: of the soul as conditioned by the experience of the flesh, of the collected experience of the living person as moulded through the relationships of the world. The resurrected are not ethereal spirits, that is to say, or part of an anonymous cloud of beings however blessed, but the same people they were in life, yet raised from imperfection and purged of corruption. The words of Jesus himself indicate that, as there is no marriage or giving in marriage in the life after death (Luke 20.35), there can be no familial or social association as in the world. The state of blessedness is not to be imagined as a kind of sanctified earth; nor is blessedness to be sought through any human yearning for consolation or survival, but for its own sake. 'My Lord, I do not love you because I hope for heaven', St Francis Xavier affirmed, 'nor yet because those who do not love you are lost eternally.'

JUSTIFICATION BY FAITH

The extent of human depravity is such that sinfulness renders acts of righteousness ambiguous. Even the most altruistic endeavours of men and women are ultimately flawed in their moral or spiritual character. The mercy of God, however, is such that corruption is overcome not by the achievement of moral rectitude but by right *belief*. It is the person who struggles to *believe* in God and the operations of his providence who attains the promise of blessedness, and the morally pure who may secure a human sufficiency which ends in itself — acquiring, in the process, the empty approval of human society. Hence the great paradox of the Christian religion: that the sinful are elected to paradise while the virtuous, who have their reward in worldly praise, may be left unenriched. This is a teaching of the Faith which the conventional piety of each age finds difficult to appreciate. But of the two men who went into the Temple to pray, it was the self-confessed sinner who was commended by Christ, and the formally religious whose reward was immediate and valueless (Luke 18.10). Translated rather starkly into the moral currency of the modern world, it is the person convicted of some despised crime who may, because of his striving for faith, be accorded the promise of eternity while the person with correct opinions and a laudable moral record who may be a pauper in spiritual terms. Here, then, is another example of the priority of the spiritual over the material, of the crucial axiom that it is what a person *believes*, rather than a record of worldly achievement, which has eternal significance. Christianity is a religion for sinners. It is, additionally, a religion for those who are educational under-achievers, or those whose minds have been stunted through limited social opportunity, or who are incapable, as St Paul testified, to manage to do the good they would really like to do (Romans 7.19). Everyone can seek faith and believe in the salvation offered by Christ. Salvation cannot be earned; it is a gift of God. We are made righteous by 'the merit of our Lord and Saviour Jesus Christ by Faith, and not for our own works or deservings' (Article XI). Authentic faith open to all people is hard to achieve, however, whereas approved moral conduct, the harbinger of worldly approval and advancement, is more easily attained — at least to the level of achievement society is conventionally likely to appreciate. Trusting in the God who is invisible, except to the eye of faith, is difficult to sustain on a daily basis and throughout the frightening vicissitudes of life; fulfilling the social requirements of moral rectitude, though not without problems, is attainable with reasonable frequency. The greatest of the sins is failure to trust in the providence of God, which is what Jesus meant when he told those who would achieve the way of understanding to take no thought for their lives, and to trust in God to provide those things necessary for his will to be done (Matthew 6.27).

MINISTRY IN THE CHURCH

The grace of God and the salvific benefits of Christ are mediated through all Christian believers, who collectively constitute the body of the Lord in the world and who are, in consequence, a royal priesthood. However important the ministry of sharing the presence of Christ, the cultivation of mutual responsibility for human welfare, the reconciliation of estranged parties, and the pursuit of a just society, it is nevertheless the transmission of the knowledge of salvation itself, and the honour due to God, which are at the centre of Christian ministry. It is in its very essence a ministry of teaching. This requires, of course, the necessary preliminary of identifying the essentials of Christian truth in a manner appropriate to the circumstances of each time and place, and of defining ways of separating various accretions which are, though often in themselves valid, no longer authentic statements of Christ's message. The body of Christian believers as the body of Christ has, then, the prior and supreme obligation to teach the knowledge entrusted to it: what the world will know of God will be what it conveys. All believers, priestly and lay, are called to this vocation.

The sacred ministry, as preserved from apostolic and historic forms within the Church of England, consists of bishops, priests and deacons, in the ordained ministry, and an increasingly articulated range of service within the lay ministry. The notion that the clergy are characteristically a learned calling is an accident of time and location, and it is likely that the intellectual gifts of the laity, in the immediate future, may well exceed those of the ordained ministers. The distinctions within sacred vocations are not recognized by conventional tests of educational achievement but by function and discipline. Priesthood is a sacrificial ministry, and those who undertake it are deprived of many alternatives, of lifestyle, for example, or of the capability of changing professional avocation. Priests also exist in a direct submission to the authority of the episcopate, and to that extent surrender freedoms which are now conventionally claimed in the lay world as ordinary civil liberties. In Anglican practice, priests are allowed to marry — this is a matter of discipline, and not of doctrine, and so may vary according to circumstance. However much they engage with the customs of society, priests are in a special sense set aside from it, however. One of the sacraments, the Holy Communion, may only be celebrated by a person in priest's orders, and this is a recognition that a distinctive mediatory function attaches to those who are called to stand in the priestly line. Christ himself appointed the twelve, and then sent out seventy-two, as the archetype of the priesthood of the new covenant: those who would deny conventional living in order to extend the Kingdom, taking neither 'purse nor scrip', the symbols of dependence on worldly provision (Luke 10.4). They are the servants of Christ and the servants of those whom Christ loves — the whole of humanity, that is to say. Bishops are priests who are primarily pastors to the pastors, and have stewardship of the general ministry. The Church is not a democratic polity, and priests are under obligation to be obedient to the direction of the episcopate. Arrangements for deciding ecclesiastical policy in a number of areas may, however, as at the present time, in practice be shared between bishops, priests, and the laity, in a series of deliberative assemblies which emulate the democratic institutions of the secular world. Priests, then, are distinctive because they are commissioned to celebrate the great final Supper of the Lord, and to administer his authority in the forgiveness of sins. They are regarded as separated from the general body of the believers not by virtue of special insights or prophetic gifts, nor by proven abilities of leadership or skills in teaching — qualities found equally in the lay ministry — but by being the immediate representatives of Christ. They are the substitutes of God himself in the performance of specific sacramental acts. In virtually all the classic religions the great mysteries disclosed to the initiates are entrusted to a priestly company solely designated for the purpose.

Lay ministry is not secondary to priestly: it is as important and necessary, but it is different in kind touching those central functions. In most areas of ministry, as in pastoral care, for example, the responsibilities of lay and clerical are identical. It is also true that lay ministry requires as much personal discipline, though expressed differently, as the priestly. The intellectual expression of Christian truth has always had an effective contribution from the laity, too (in some early heresies, like the Donatist schism of the fourth century, it was the bishops who erred and the laity who remained faithful).

It has become the practice of the

Church of England to admit women to the order of priesthood.

THE DOCTRINE OF THE CHURCH

According to Latin and Greek (Catholic and Orthodox) tradition the *magisterium*, the teaching office of the Church is incapable of error over the definition of essential doctrines. This derives from the application of the words of Christ, when he promised that the Holy Spirit would keep his followers faithful in truth (John 14.26). Indefectibility does not, according to this understanding, extend to all pronouncements of Christian leaders or bodies, but to definitions made by General Councils of the Church — assemblies drawn from the whole world — and in practice has applied to a relatively small number of doctrinal statements. All other teaching definitions may vary in their form and application according to circumstance, provided always that they are consonant with received interpretations of Scripture and Tradition. The matter is absolutely crucial, and it is no accident that it is differences over the doctrine of the Church which form the centres of disagreement between the Christian Churches. It has to do with the very means by which authority is determined: how truth is known to be true.

The Church of England explicitly denies the existence of an indefectible *magisterium*, and holds that General Councils of the Church, including the seminal early Councils which defined the core doctrines of Christianity, are capable of error, and, as a matter of historical record, have in fact erred (Articles XIX, XXI). Anglicans also insist on the priority of Scriptural over Traditional authority, pointing out that the Churches of the early period, too, had erred 'not only in their living and manner of Ceremonies, but also in matters of Faith' (Article XIX). Vigorous denial of the indefectibility of Councils, and therefore of the *magisterium*, taken together with the principle of the autonomy of national Churches, identifies the Church of England as belonging fundamentally to the Protestant tradition of Christianity — and such, indeed, has at most times in its history been its claim. Yet the Church has in recent decades come to regard itself as annexed to a wider body — a universal Church of many branches or representations, described in the Preface to the Declaration of Assent in the Ordinal (1973–4, 1980) as 'the one, holy, catholic, and apostolic Church, worshipping the one true God, Father, Son, and Holy Spirit', and whose beliefs are rendered in 'the catholic creeds'. It is, however, unclear exactly how this wider Church is to be understood. Perhaps it is as a spiritualized quasi-federation of episcopal denominations; or is it intended to incorporate any trinitarian body which appears to be regularly constituted?

There is, then, still a need for the Church of England to have an authoritative teaching office, and for clarity about exactly what happened when the Church separated from the authority of Rome — and from the ability to attend General Councils — at the time of the English Reformation in the sixteenth century. The immediate practice thereafter was Erastian: the subordination of ecclesiastical order to the authority of the state. But it was never held that this extended to matters of doctrine, though the Crown was able to determine what the *existing* doctrines of the Church of England were in the event of disputation (a function for many years of the Judicial Committee of the Privy Council). The revival in 1970 of synodical government within the Church does not clarify the issue of authority. Synods do not, in Christian tradition, define doctrine — and anyway the Anglican synods sit ultimately by authority of Parliament (as a Church established by law). In the history of the western Church synods have been concerned with matters of order, discipline, and local use. It is only General Councils which define doctrine, even in the understanding of the Church of England, which has no access to them. The Worship and Doctrine Measure promulged by the General Synod in 1975 would appear to express a capability to determine *doctrine*, but this presumably refers to the construction or interpretation of existing formularies and not to any capacity to initiate changes or additions. According to its formularies the Church of England accepts the validity of the doctrinal definitions made in Councils held before the

Reformation whilst simultaneously confessing that in some things their decrees were erroneous. Under Article XXI those acts of Councils may be received which are not contrary to Scripture. There is no guidance about how to arrive at an authoritative interpretation of Scripture, however.

In recent decades many Anglicans have been attracted to an informal ecclesiology known as 'dispersed authority'. This envisages a plurality of approaches to Christian truth, with no single tradition of believers enjoying a primacy. Truthful and erroneous understandings of the Faith coexist in a fruitful dialectical relationship — a description, not of the ideal but of existing realities — which, judged over time and comparatively, can be said to evolve as the mind of Christ. It is the dynamics of Providence which thus further Christian understanding, rather than the more static decrees of conciliar bodies or an authoritative *magisterium*. This notion has at least one affinity with the Catholic concept of development of doctrine: it recognizes a progressive advance of truth, with the People of God disclosing new dimensions of the splendour of the divine dispensation in each age and place.

With no overt doctrine of the Church, however, there needs to be a clear practical operation of a machinery of authority in order to identify error. It may be possible to conclude that all doctrine necessary for salvation was established before the Reformation, but this certainly does not obviate the continuing need for a means of combating what used to be called heresy, or false doctrine. An organism needs not only internal defence against disease but protection against infection from outside — faith needs to be combined with vigilance. The world has always been filled with ideas and practices which are intrinsically hostile to Christ's teaching, and these often present to society a benign and apparently wholesome face. It is the errors which most plainly are such which least need identification. The existence of authority in the Church, therefore, is absolutely essential not only for the definition of truth but for the avoidance of evil. Only thus can Christ's little ones be safeguarded against the forces which might cause them to stumble.

II

Morality and Applications

MORAL FOUNDATIONS

Christian *doctrines* are unchanging. They are concerned with the nature of God and his relationship to the creation. *Morality*, however, involves dealings between people in the world, the conduct of economic and social life, and the personal use of the body as the earthly vehicle of the soul: matters which show a measure of contingency as times change and understanding, both of moral law and of change itself, undergo transformation. It is arguable that *new* doctrines may be added to the original deposit — by those who embrace concepts of development, and whose view of doctrinal definition relates it to an organic concept of the *magisterium* — but moral understanding is always in a process of development. Even adhesion to a fixed body of moral law, as within Christianity, plainly admits also that law needs to relate to custom and social use in order for it to be effected in actual lives. Jesus himself showed this to be the case in his prescription. He said of some moral law that 'it was written of old time' and added 'but I say to you' (Matthew 5.21) — thereby disclosing not only his own authority over moral law (the main purport of the saying) but the need to adjust morality to changed understanding. This is a difficult area. Believers have themselves rarely agreed about what constitutes the permanent aspect of a moral teaching and what part of its application can be legitimately regarded as contingent. Although originally delivered to quasi-nomadic peoples, however, Judaic morality transcended the conditions of the desert: it derived from earlier folk experience through which certain essentials of conduct had already been refined, and it later adapted itself to the circumstances of exile and rule by others. Like all moral law, the traditions which came into Christianity had themselves been subject to dynamic changes produced by dialectical exchanges with a number of external moral ideas. So the providence of God acts through the complicated circumstances of his involvement with human history. By far the larger part of Christian morality and moral sense is shared with the common moralities of the ancient world, and may, perhaps, best be described as a compilation of ordinary 'decent' and ordered behaviour. It is sometimes said today that Christian morality has been the foundation of the kind of human 'decency' expressed in secular humanism; but this is not really the case — it is Christian morality itself which incorporates the commonplaces of 'decency' in personal relationships which are general to humanity and which, for some, including the medieval Christian philosophers, furnish evidence for the existence of Natural Law. St Paul referred to a universal knowledge in just this sense (Acts 17.24–28). If Christianity is reduced to its ethical content only, as some moralists have attempted in the past two centuries, then it appears distinctly unoriginal.

Moral behaviour is not conduct which is necessarily *good* behaviour. To be moral is to behave according to a structured and predictable code or system. If the code or system is corrupt, wholly or in part, then the consequent moral conduct will be unacceptable to Christians: it is the *content* of morality, for them, and its sovereign source, which matters. And Christians do believe that there exists a code and system of moral law established by God himself. It derived originally from his providential education of all peoples into elementary styles of ordered living, and then of the Jewish people into the conditions of a sufficiently articulated set of moral prescriptions as to form the basis of a covenant with God. The Ten Commandments are an absolutely essential statement of moral law, true in all circumstances. The images used, of course, require expression today in ways more applicable to modern society (coveting a neighbour's ox or ass, for example, is better rendered as coveting his means of livelihood, and so forth). In deciding what part or aspect of moral law is permanent, and what changes with altered circumstance, is not easy. It is tempting to go back to sources, and to recreate, for analysis, the conditions in which certain laws were originally found necessary, and to determine that the conduct now considered unlawful, was then understood quite differently. Concepts as well as words change their meaning over time. The problem with returning to origins, however, is that religious belief is itself not static, and brings forth things both new and old. A moral insight now held for good reason — observation of human behaviour in the light of modern social knowledge, for example — but which appears contrary to received and ancient moral wisdom, could well be a legitimate development and not a corruption made for purposes of contemporary convenience. Or it may not be. Humans have a record of self-deception when it comes to moral justification of surrender to desire. It is also true that those who today reject the concept of development in relation to doctrinal definition may well accept it over moral issues. Liberal Protestants are often within this category of believers. Yet for all this it must surely be helpful to examine the conditions in which moral law had its origins in order to help determine what the moral teaching of the religious tradition actually is — provided such an exploration is not regarded as unilaterally decisive.

There is a whole class of moral definition which has no basis in past experience, particularly concerning such matters as medical ethics, manipulation of organic materials, the use of technology, the presentation of information, the extension of public responsibility for welfare provision, extra-cosmic exploration, and cultural relativism. In such matters, inherited Christian moral understanding needs to be reduced to its largest principles so that these may in turn be reapplied in the novel conditions. This is an exercise which is probably beneficial in itself, since it encourages a precision of thought, and an emancipation from immediate cultural assumptions, which can surely only tend to the discovery of truth. And God is by definition all truth. The question still remains, however, as to the extent to which humanity, called by its discoveries to join with God in the progressive development of the planet, encounters limits ordained by God. Moral law is also about deciding how far people may go if the eventual results of their action may produce perversions of the divine scheme rather than enhancements of it. In these circumstances reference back to the inherent depravity of human nature becomes essential. Moral law is required precisely because conditions exist — indeed they are commonplace — when individual passion and self-seeking override restraint and altruism. On such occasions law exists to obviate the need for instantaneous moral decision: a code of reference exists to provide the individual with the proper course of action. Moral law, for these reasons, has objective reality; it is not 'the situation' which provides its own moral explanation but fixed principles of behaviour which are brought to bear upon the reality of individual lives. Christianity believes that there are fixed laws, founded upon divinely-revealed principles, and in realistic correspondence to the unpleasing facts of human moral frailty. It also believes that a lesser category of moral law exists, no less binding, which is capable of change as the world changes or as it comes to recognize that its previous understanding of things was disordered because of insufficient knowledge available to earlier law-makers. Christians would have grave difficulty in adducing a sliding scale to determine which laws are immutable and which are contingent were it not for the divine mission of the Holy Spirit — which is to preserve them in all truth. Christian moral life indicates the presence of the Spirit; it describes providence in real operation in the world. Thus law, in Christian understanding, and in correspondence with the teaching of Christ himself, is not a matter of constraints and negatives (as its formal tabulation might suggest) but a means of releasing believers to recognize and practise the spirituality for which they were created.

IMMUTABLE MORAL LAW

The Ten Commandments were given directly by God, and are unchangeable. Covetousness, therefore, and murder or adultery, are always sinful if committed in the plain and ordinary sense of the words. Of course there may be situations of conflict in which military deaths may be classified by some as murders, and the definition of adultery made flexible by the conditions which prompted the dissolution of a marriage — there will always be parties, either to warfare or to marital strife, who will wish to represent their innocence. But in most circumstances the plain meaning of the Commandments can be received without ambiguity. The moral exhortations of Christ form the second great basis of Christian law, and the morality deduced from them, too, is absolutely binding for believers. There is, in Christ's teaching, no systematic moral system, however. This is partly because he assumed the continuation, with some adjustments, of the old Jewish law, and partly because the main body of his own moral exhortation came in the form of parables — whose chief purpose was the revelation of divine authority rather than the construction of systematic ethics. The Church has formulated moral law out of the sayings of Christ, nevertheless, and, because it has the authority of Christ himself, and because the scriptural account of his words is believed to be accurate (as statements of the intention of his teaching), this moral law is absolutely unchanging. When Jesus declared that it was moral to perform acts of healing on the sabbath day, for example (Luke 14.1), his words became as applicable now as they were in the Herodian era.

Christian morality is neither derived nor applied because of the social consequences of actions, or because certain courses of action may be productive of more pleasure than pain, but because of the intrinsic effect on the dignity of the person, as one called to be in a relationship with God. Moral law is true in itself, and respect for it concerns the nature of the human person and spiritual formation; moral actions are not primarily enjoined because of possible social utility, in Christian understanding, but because they are required by God as a necessary expression of the existence of the Kingdom.

POLITICAL MORALITY

The history of the Church shows that it has always considered its own mission as compatible with many different forms of political order, from the Roman *imperium* to Western liberal democracy. The emphasis has been on the existence of *order*, the conditions of stability and protection in which morality can be practised. There has been a long debate amongst Christian thinkers about the means by which order and the political authority necessary for its maintenance may be defined as having legitimacy. Tyranny, or unjust exercise of power, needs to be recognized in very precise ways, or anarchy may result by the actions of individuals or social groups whose unilateral identification of unwarranted power is allowed free expression. Christians have in general contended that government is just, not where it depends upon particular political devices to come into existence or to preserve itself, or because it rests on consent, but where it can be shown to preserve order, to protect moral life, and to defend society from external assault. There is no requirement for the morality or the religion of government to be that of a majority of the citizens, since, as a matter of fact, human society, except where unduly coerced, exists in a condition of divided opinion on these matters, and nothing in political experience suggests that a majority is likely, in its nature, to be right. The problem is that traditional political authority was regarded as being entrusted with the propagation of truth — and usually employed a Church or a clerical caste to provide institutional machinery for the task. Opinion which was not in correspondence with the official body of ideas suffered a loss of liberties, a condition acceptable since it was held, even by those whose beliefs were not recognized, that it was the duty of the state to propagate truth. Hence the use of force to change the religion of the state: this was sometimes internal, but more commonly, in the history of the world, occurred as a result of warfare. Such a condition is no longer tolerable to modern judgement, which now contends, anyway, for the notion of a 'plural' society. The state is today envisaged as a balancing mechanism, responsive to majority direction (at least in terms of legitimizing its authority), whose obligation is to preside over a series of competing religions and moral groups. The essential functions of order and defence remain. The modern state, however, is quite different in kind from its traditional predecessors, since it has come to acquire collectivist functions. These huge additional powers, largely added in the interests of securing and enhancing the material welfare of the citizens, rest on an undefined moral basis and yet are paradoxically perceived to be moral in nature. Christians conventionally identify them as being inherently Christian — the love of neighbour — yet at the same time would decline to regard it as the duty of the state to impose morality because it is by nature Christian. It is no longer regarded as an obligation for the state that it should be seen as having the capacity to identify religious truth and to enforce it. Indeed, such a function would now be regarded as unjust, since it would fail to recognize the existence of the general pluralism of values. The whole area is rarely addressed with any religious or philosophical coherence, and as modern welfare collectivism appears to lack a systematic moral basis, and depends, instead, on a species of calculated hedonism, the Church has in practice offered its own commentary on *particular* issues, raised *ad hoc* in general political discourse, without attempting an integrated analysis. In common debate many church leaders have endorsed political democracy, but democracy is a device and not a moral basis: few, presumably, would seriously claim that moral or spiritual truth can properly be determined by the counting of heads. The most obvious way of conducting government in a society of genuinely competing moral or religious opinion is to reduce the level of activity of the state, so lowering the number of decisions in which reference has to be made to a moral foundation. But in the end all acts of government, because they ultimately rest on force to be effective, require moral justification, and the rise of the collectivist state, anyway, with its heightened public expectations, makes a significant reduction of the sphere of state action in present circumstances quite unrealistic. It seems set, on the contrary, to expand still further.

The Church of England has been faithful to the teaching of Christ himself (Mark 12.17) and of St Paul (Romans 13.1) in accepting the legitimacy of duly constituted political authority, even when, as in the experience of the first Christians, that authority was hostile to the Church. Both the historical conditions which accompanied the changes of the English Reformation, and subsequent constitutional development, required the Church of England, as a national establishment of religion, to teach the loyalty of subjects to the Crown. To this day dignitaries of the Church take oaths of allegiance to political authority as a condition of entering office, rendered in terms of allegiance to the Crown. To that extent it may be said that the Church of England endorses the monarchical form of government — as it has evolved into a constitutional order resting on democratic practice in the selection of members of the functioning executive and legislature. The right of civil authority to order the affairs of the Church is admitted in Articles XXI, XXXV, XXXVI and XXXVII. Legislation devolving authority to synods set up under ecclesiastical authority has since 1970, however, rendered many of these powers highly formal, and the Church, which has since the Reformation been characterized by an emphatically erastian polity, may now be said to be in practice free of political control. There is no officially sanctioned body of Church teaching which endorses any particular form of government, but a lengthy series of reports and decisions of ecclesiastical bodies has, during the last century, produced material from which a set of conclusions may be inferred, and which could be said to have a kind of working authority. From these it may be seen that the Church of England identifies representative political democracy to be the most available and realistic form of political association which has a sympathetic moral basis. That basis recognizes the individual worth of each citizen and the capacity of each to have a voice in public affairs. The Church acclaims the existence of a plural society as one in which there is diversity of moral choice, which it identifies as good in itself, and believes that those components of the plurality which accept democratic procedures should be admitted to political participation. It shares the prevailing opinion that the views of those who are hostile to the shared common morality (racists, for example) should be illegal if given public expression. It believes that law should encourage moral opinion regarded as correct in relation to specified issues of the times, and that it should furnish sanctions against incorrect moral opinion — as well as performing conventional functions of preserving order. It accepts the widening collectivist concerns of government as being an indication of moral advance. It regards it as necessary in public authority that it should provide for a just distribution of resources and for more equitable relationships in the terms of work.

In declining to see Christianity and Christian morality imposed by law, and in endorsing the notion that a common shared morality exists among civilized people, the Church of England shows an adhesion to modern liberalism on the one hand, with its opposition to favour being granted to one religious body over another by the state, and to a sort of latter-day Natural Law theory on the other. This second concept remains undefined; yet it has interesting resonances with past Christian endorsement of Natural Law morality, in the Aristotelian and Thomist traditions — in the case of the Church of England transmitted largely through the writings of Hooker (died 1600). If a common shared morality really does exist in modern England, and has a firm and identifiable theoretical basis, then its exploration by Christian apologists could well advance understanding of the attitudes which believers should take to issues of the day. But if the familiar rhetoric of moral agreement merely describes a transient moment in the exchange between traditional Christian morality and secular humanism — with the latter plainly advancing — then Christians should be wary of associating themselves too convincedly with prevailing moral pieties, since they could prove unstable.

Implicit in all this is the rejection by the modern Church of the old 'Christendom' model: that Christian truth should be protected and extended by the control and use of the machinery of the state, where possible on an exclusive basis. Although such a model now seems illiberal to Church leaders, however, it might be noticed that it continues to be the method promoted for the advance of their own ideals by secular ideological and moral rivals.

ECONOMIC AND SOCIAL ORDER

As in its relationship to political organization the Church has, since its beginning,
shown itself compatible with a wide range of
economic practices and social orderings.
Today it broadly accepts the virtues of
capitalist enterprise, suitably regulated by
agencies of public authority; for centuries, in
contrast, it condemned the practice of usury
which lies at the basis of the free-market
system. Once the Church taught the necessary acceptance of a graded and ordered
society, as required to preserve the most
fundamental of social values; today it is
highly critical of social inequality. And as,
again, with political morality, the Church of
England has no authoritative body of teaching in this area, its advice to its members and
its signals to the world have to be constructed from Anglican resolutions and from
synodical reports — many of which explicitly declare that they sustain only the
authority of their immediate authors. (The
proceedings of Lambeth Conferences are
only advisory, and begin to apply to church
members only as each Province of the

Communion separately resolves to adopt them with such machinery of authority as it believes itself possessed.) But Christians are plainly obliged by their Faith to be concerned with economic and social issues, since they form the area in which the love of neighbour commanded by God and repeated by Christ has its actual expression. Christian love of neighbour, furthermore, is taken to have a collective meaning, and not to apply merely in dealings between individuals. Acceptance of the morality of the modern collectivist state implies also full acceptance of the hugely enhanced power of the state to intervene, on grounds of social justice, in economic relationships. It also prompts Christians to approve of attempts by public authority to contrive social provisions to alleviate the consequences of poverty and improvidence. Christianity, that is to say, is as insistent now as it has always been in understanding religious practice to involve a high degree of individual participation in the creation of a just society. It is the definition of social justice which has changed over time, not the exhortation of church authorities to their adherents that they have an obligation to be involved.

The Church of England teaches that an approved conduct of economic activity must tend to the creation of wealth which is as widely available to members of society as is technically compatible with effective wealth-creating processes. The means of production, distribution and exchange, whether under private or public ownership, should be arranged with a definite moral end: justice in society. This implies, for example, the legitimacy of the organization of labour; of reasonable profits for those who risk capital; a regulation by public authority of wages and conditions of labour; statutory control of minimum requirements for terms of employment to secure dignity in labour; provision for health and safety; decent housing; holiday benefits; protection for investors in private enterprises; fair taxation (which, to achieve what may be considered fairness, may include a redistributive element); access to transport; protection for savings. The Church of England also endorses social provision, including a public health service, with its attendant and ancillary benefits; state pensions for the elderly and disadvantaged; guaranteed payments to those who are sick; education at the public expense; free and equal access to justice; the discouraging in ordinary circumstances of capital punishment; support for measures to foster racial and sexual equality; measures which recognize the advantages of social diversity where this is beneficial to the whole society. There are some important areas in which the Church declines to offer advice to its members, such as, for example, whether state economic enterprise is to be considered preferable to private enterprise as a general theoretical proposition, or the extent to which the state should become involved in the sponsorship of religious or moral institutions — the historic Establishment of the Church of England itself being, in these days, largely defended on utilitarian grounds. Few now contend that the state has the capacity to identify religious truth and to recognize Anglicanism as its embodiment: which was the traditional basis of establishment — rather than the contention that the Church of England enjoyed a majority support in society. The Church has also declined to express a modern version or reconsideration of its traditional support of social hierarchy. Its leading figures have long been especially sceptical of some inequalitarian features of class society. No systematic alternative has been suggested, however, despite the clear preference of the mind of the Church for a social ideal more commensurate with social justice as conventionally received in modern England.

Modern church writers have frequently adhered to a distinction, in economic and social issues, between general principles and particular applications. The Church collectively, through its consultative or governmental institutions, should, it is held, define the grand principles of moral action, defined by reference to theological learning, but that particular applications — actual policy — should be the province of the lay world with its expertise in the various fields of enterprise. Distinctions of this nature were most clearly argued by William Temple (d. 1944), and have received acceptance through his distinguished advocacy. Despite the apparent ease with which such distinctions could be applied, however, the matter remains fraught with difficulties — not the least of which derive from the massive growth of the collectivist powers of the state since Temple's day, and from the consequent diminution of clarity between principles which have become applications in a primary stage of state advance, and applications made later which then appear to have the character of principles. A dialectic operating according to escalating government dynamics on the scale now commonplace is neither easy to discern nor practical to control.

In economic and social order, as in its view of political organization and morality, the Church of England may be seen to be in broad sympathy with the aims of modern liberal democracy. It does not, however, consider this polity as an ideal form of government, regarding it only as a commendable vehicle for Christian service in present circumstances.

STEWARDSHIP OF THE EARTH

The creation myths in the Book of Genesis make it quite clear that humanity was given lordship over the living things of the earth. Animals and birds and 'everything that moves on the ground' and fish in the sea, God told Noah, 'I give them all to you, as I have given you every green plant' (Genesis 9.2–3). It was a limited lordship, nevertheless, established in the nature of humanity itself as part of the animal creation — capable of being compared 'to the beasts that perish' (Psalm 49.12) — despite the divinely ordered qualities of reason and reflection. Although at the disposal of humans, it is precisely because of their innocence of reflective choice that animals cannot be treated without moral consideration. They are, so to say, held in the same kind of trusteeship by men and women as is the entire planet. Humanity is thus answerable to God for use made of the resources of the earth, including its animal life. The relationship of humans to animal life has by its nature to be one-sided, however, since the moral reflection which provides the guiding principle belongs to one of the parties only. This should enhance rather than diminish the entry of moral judgement in decisions which have to be made, both individually and collectively, about animals and other living things. Yet the first duty of humanity is its own perpetuation, to fulfil God's providential scheme. The first purpose of animal and plant life, accordingly, is to provide human sustenance. Modern people, with their detached urban mentality, often find the concept of animal creation as primarily a food resource somewhat crude; but it is the way the world was established, and whether we like it or not living things, including humans, exist in an everlasting process of mutual absorption — the food chain. Living things do not only provide sustenance, they also occasion disease. It is microscopic units of living matter (bacteria, viruses) which may cause harm as well as good to the effective operation of the human body, and although moral constraints obviously do not operate in encouraging their presence or attempting to eradicate them, according to their effects, there still remain moral considerations about the manner in which manipulation of living matter may be conducted. These raise fundamental issues about the *extent* to which humans are called to join with God in the development of life itself. Here is a difficult area, where the questions raised are themselves still unclear — in what is a rapidly evolving dimension of human knowledge about the mechanics of the Creation. People are not consistent in their attitudes to non-human life, positing a moral dimension in their relationship to animals, but not regarding microscopic forms of life as possessed of qualities calling for moral consideration. In the controversial area of the manipulation of life itself much is made of 'ethical' debate in the various public bodies who set up the terms of reference. Yet there is little attempt to define the pedigree or origin of the ethical code whose precepts are presumably being applied — and it usually turns out that by 'ethical' commentators actually mean whatever serves the purpose of alleviating human suffering or in some manner enhances what is perceived to be the quality of human life. The Church does not equate goodness with human satisfaction, and regards all manipulation of the primary materials of human life as necessarily subject to extreme restraint. For Christians, the purpose of any act of biological engineering should be the furtherance of God's perfection in his Creation, and not an attempt to re-create life according to human design.

Human responsibility for the material resources of the planet is more lucidly explicable. Scriptural inferences indicate that the earth is to be exploited by humans, for their immediate sustenance and, by examination of its nature and composition, for intellectual advance. It is clearly not in furtherance of the divine scheme that the data for human enrichment should itself be used improvidently and without moral consideration for the needs of future generations. The modern movements for ecological seriousness and conservation, despite the romanticism to which they are occasionally given, are fully consonant with a Christian understanding of the world and have, indeed, developed largely within cultures which are historically indebted to a Christian inheritance.

WARFARE

Despite the respect pacifism has in general been accorded within the Christian tradition, most Christian believers, and church authorities, have considered armed conflict a legitimate manner of defending righteous causes and of protecting what are perceived to be innocent parties. In classical political theory the state itself was a divine institution, providing the coercion necessary to allow morality to flourish — and that implied the use of force in even small-scale matters of civil order. It has been the *conditions* of prosecuting warfare which have most exercised Christian moralists: the calculation of scale, effectiveness, permitted levels of violence and punitive intent. In the twentieth century some Christian thinkers attempted a revival of the so-called 'Just War' theories current in medieval Christendom. This resulted in a number of useful insights, but the type of warfare which in the modern world accompanies attrition between collectivist states, and the prevalence of democratic politics (which renders the people morally responsible for the actions of their governments), as well as the scale of the destructive potential of weaponry, have made these early theories — which operated in such small-scale societies — difficult to apply today. The Church of England has been sensitive to the new issues raised by the invention of nuclear weapons, and has shown itself, in its several declarations on the matter, opposed to their use but not opposed to their possession by sovereign states as a means of deterrence. The concept of 'innocent' civilian victims in modern warfare is difficult to maintain, however, in the light of democratic consent to the war aims of governments. The Church believes that all warfare only becomes legitimate after negotiation between the opposed parties, where conditions allow them, have failed to reach settlement or accommodation. Subsequent military undertakings, it also contends, should be proportionate to the ends sought and conducted with minimum loss of life or damage to life-sustaining infrastructure.

SEXUAL MORALITY

It has become commonplace to consider the Church, and especially the Victorian Church, to have had an over-restrictive or censorious view of human sexuality. Yet human sexuality is an important and un-avoidable area of Christian moral teaching: it is central to God's providential scheme for the perpetuation of the species; it provides the most familiar and frequent occasion for individual moral choice; it is one of the most testing passions which involve mastery over the body and therefore over personal desire; it is an expression of human affection and love. The Church has always promoted chastity as a cardinal Christian ideal not because it is a denial of any of these primary purposes of sexuality but because it is a perfect offering of self-sacrifice. All moral law exists to be efficacious where the emotions might overrule reason in actual situations of choice; law in relation to sexual behaviour is especially necessary since the passions then experienced are particularly strong — and in situations of love inevitably appear to present the individual with emotions which seem unique.

Modern thinking, and the behavioural, biological, and anthropological knowledge upon which its most telling contributions are based, has offered so much that is new in attitudes to sexuality as to amount to a revolution. Some of this thought contains valuable insights which can inform the application of moral law. Thus many sexual impulsions formerly attributed to personal choice or wilful corruption can now be recognized as due to conditioning beyond the control of the person: some biological or even genetic, some germane to early environmental experience. Areas of modern thought, on the other hand, can be dangerously relativizing, and if allowed to develop without moral guidelines would issue in moral nihilism. The intellectual capability of the thinker does not release him or her from the distorting effects of sexual desire. Advances in understanding the nature of sexuality, however, may be regarded as part of the general calling of men and women to share in the progressive development of life, and are to be welcomed accordingly and explained within the context of the Christian tradition. Misuse of sexuality, or wilful misunderstanding of the need for moral law in relation to sexuality, is a grave decline in human dignity, subordinating the higher instincts of the person to the lower, and incapacitating spiritual formation through the surrender of ordered living. Mastery of the self is a primary Christian obligation (1 Thessalonians 4.4).

The Church of England believes that human sexuality is most properly expressed within heterosexual married life. Other forms of sexual practice, though not necessarily sinful, are regarded as impaired or 'falling short of the Christian ideal'. This teaching indicates the priority of the pro-creation of children as the primary end of sexuality, yet it does not exclude sexual passion as being an accompaniment of relationships of love in a wider sense. For Anglicans, however, heterosexual congress remains the form of sexual expression which most regularly discloses God's will for humanity, and its practice exclusively within the married state is not only a guarantee of fidelity but also the provision of the family unit which the Church believes to be the most desirable manner of socializing and moralizing children. This second end of marriage is happily accomplished where the mutual affection of parents develops within conditions of stability and security which marriage, where successful, achieves. It should be noticed, however, that in traditional society, and also in compatibility with the teaching of the Church, marriage was a social arrangement in which experiences of romantic love were not routinely expected. The close family unit, with its ideal of shared activity and sympathetic values, is largely a modern concept — and the rising levels of divorce could well indicate that it is not, as an ideal, always realistically compatible with modern expectations to individuality of choice.

The marriage discipline. The Church of England teaches that marriage is indissoluble, and that divorce is in no circumstances acceptable. This derives not only from the sayings of Christ (and despite his apparent acceptance of adultery as a ground of divorce in St Matthew's Gospel 19.9), but also and primarily from the oaths taken in marriage by the partners. These state plainly that the bond exists 'for better or for worse', and attempts at dissolution therefore constitute a species of perjury. Where the practical breakdown of a marriage requires separation, in order to preserve the partners from the moral hazards of mutual hatred, the

obligations undertaken in the original contract survive in relation to the social effects
of the marriage. Sexual relations with other
partners, thereafter, constitute adultery. The
concepts of 'innocent' or 'guilty' parties in a
marriage dissolution, practical or legal,
which have now been removed from secular
law, look increasingly unrealistic as a basis
for church moral law, since culpability, once
removed from a legal frame of reference, is
extremely difficult to determine. The
Church has therefore retained its complete
ban on all divorce, for its own members, in
recognition of practical as well as moral
considerations. There are also spiritual
reasons: the form of marriage used in the
Church of England compares the relationship of the partners with that of Christ and
his Church. Mindful, however, of its pastoral
relationship to its own members, and conscious of the difficulties faced by those many
Anglicans who do as a matter of fact get
divorced, the Church of England is seeking
ways of remarrying divorced people in
Church. Marriage is not a sacrament in the
understanding of the Church of England, but
it has qualities which are like a sacrament in

their intention. Arrangements whereby heterosexual partners decide to live together outside marriage are not approved by the Church, largely because they would appear to ignore the commitment and security which marriage enjoins. Such liaisons, now common in society, are not in themselves unchristian if the partners involved intend moral prescription in all other dimensions of their lives. Sexual promiscuity is not allowed by the Church, as constituting a lifestyle which is potentially corrupting to the dignity of the person. Polygamy is not allowed since it is an affront to the equality of men and women. A resolution of the Lambeth Conference of 1998, however, allowed polygamy amongst black Christians resident in countries of Africa.

Homosexuality. Christianity in the past, like most other religions, reflected in its teachings the rejection of homosexuality found in many cultures — doubtless itself derived from a disinclination to encourage, in primitive societies where humans were a scarce resource, sexual practices which inhibited reproduction. The Church continues to classify homosexuality as an intrinsically disordered condition ('against nature'), yet significant numbers of Christians are, and actually always have been, themselves homosexual. Two considerations may help to educate judgement. The first is that homosexuality is not in general chosen: it is an expression of sexuality which derives from conditions of inherited impulsions or of early infant experience, over which the individual has no control; and it may well not be a condition to be regretted but to have divinely ordered and positive qualities. The second is that what may have in the past been condemned by society and the Church is not homosexuality in itself, but certain types of depraved behaviour and excessive indulgence which, where they are found in heterosexual liaisons, are equally to be rejected by those seeking the sanctification of their whole persons. The modern Church of England has been by turns opaque and ambiguous in its expressed teaching about homosexuality, tending to suggest that there is no moral censure of this sexuality *per se* but that homosexual *practice* promotes negative moral value and is to be discouraged. The Church, in its resolutions, has also appeared to discriminate between the clergy and the laity in the standards of sexual conduct it requires. Clearly the matter must await a general redefinition of the morality of human sexuality, but until that is attempted homosexual Christian believers should be assured of the full integrity of their membership of the Church, and encouraged to find in their sexual preferences such elements of moral beauty as may enhance their general understanding of Christ's calling. It may be noted that it is these days accepted that all kinds of sexual practices, once regarded as degrading and lamentable, are routinely considered normal or even healthy expressions of sexual affection within heterosexual relationships.

Abortion. The Church of England absolutely condemns abortion in all circumstances. It is a grave sin against God's providence, since it is in his determination that life exists in the condition he ordains. Abortions performed for social reasons (to prevent the lifestyles of individuals from being adversely affected by the obligations attached to the rearing of a child) are patently evil; those carried out in order to avoid births where there may be hazard to the life of the mother or where an infant may suffer bodily defects or be liable to them later in life, though perhaps well intended, are nevertheless equally sins against providence. Christians can no more be allowed individual choice over the artificial termination of a pregnancy than they can over the extinction of any human life. Abortion was condemned at the Council of Elvira (306), and it may be assumed that this is one of the decrees of the early Councils which the Church of England has subsumed within its teaching.

Artificial means of birth control. The practice of contraception is now very widespread amongst Anglicans, and yet it was not until the Lambeth Conference of 1930 that first steps were taken to reverse the strongly adverse declarations of preceding Conferences. In 1958 the Lambeth Conference endorsed what it called 'responsible parenthood' fully recognizing a 'secondary end' in marriage, by which human sexual exchange could be seen to celebrate relationships of affection separable from the purpose of procreation. This separation, between procreative intention and sexual pleasure, seems to have found general acceptance within the Church of England, even though a number of allied theological questions remain unaddressed. It may be asked, for example, why the undoubtedly 'unnatural' interference with intercourse involved in artificial means of contraception is permissible, while other sexual practices deemed unnatural (homosexual love, oral sex) are not. Perhaps the best way of assessing the moral value of human sexual congress in which the primary procreative purpose is frustrated is to emphasize the dignity of the person. To what extent is the individual enhanced or diminished; what course tends to the elevation of the sexual act and what reduces sexual expression to a mere utility? The Church of England believes that the expression of a relationship of affection and commitment between married people remains moral where the procreative intention is suppressed in order to avoid the perceived evil of generating children for whom no satisfactory conditions of living can be anticipated. Since the Church of England simultaneously believes that sexual love can only legitimately be expressed within the marriage bond, it follows that artificial means of contraception can never be moral when employed by persons outside marriage.

THE FAMILY

When two people come together for sexual relationship, with the intention of establishing a stable bond of union, a family comes into existence. This is a matter of description, not a moral evaluation: a family may exist outside of a formally recognizable marriage contract, as in natural society, or in the more conventional married state generally approved by opinion today. It also exists whether or not there are children. Since procreation is the chief end of Christian marriage, however, it follows that unless there are physiological or biological impediments married life will ordinarily be accompanied by the wider society of children. The family, and what are commonly called 'family values', are quite separate, for the family, as such, is simply an institution or social device — the means by which *any* values are transmitted. The family does not of itself, that is to say, generate its own values; it is the means by which values coming to it from external sources — such as a tradition of belief or a shared vocabulary of morals — can be imparted to the young and experienced in actual conditions of social exchange. The small scale of family life becomes a laboratory for social life, a testing ground for the induction of successive generations into the preferred teachings to which the family members adhere. There have been many in the history of ideas who have experimented with schemes for the socializing of children in other units, some of which have been under the direct patronage of the state: but these, whatever other disadvantages they may show, have never been able to match the sheer effectiveness of the family as the most efficient means by which values are transmitted. It came as a confirmation of this, for example, that when the Soviet Union collapsed in 1990 — and despite every attempt in that society to use the influence of the state to eradicate religious belief — Christianity was found to have been handed on inside families, and re-emerged in a remarkably robust form. The chief enemy of the Faith, in modern circumstances, would appear to be not direct ideological assault but the relativizing effects of cultural secularization.

Families have rights which precede those of the state and are superior to them. First among them is the right to impart religious beliefs and practices to children inside the family compact. The modern collectivist state has made considerable intrusions into areas of family practice which once were regarded as exclusively in the right of family determination — usually in the furtherance of educational and welfare provision. The Church has no particular view as to how far these types of interferences may go, or what limits might be set to them. But it is insistent on the right of the family to teach children religious truth. With this goes the right of the Church to maintain its own educational institutions. The concept of 'family values', however, is not stable: the content of what are perceived as 'values' changes over time — especially the actual nature of family life itself, since the model currently proposed describes the middle-class aspirations of fairly prosperous Western family experience in the last century-and-a-half.

HUMAN RIGHTS

Men and women, either individually or collectively, cannot have any rights in relation to God. Rights are understood to exist when there is some perceived universal moral norm, which leads to categorization in Natural Law, or when political authority legislates and creates rights, which constitute the positive laws of states. Rights recognized in both these ways belong to the social order and are known through the discoveries of human experience over time. The divine laws, derived from revelation, though they impart obligations and not rights to humans, nevertheless set out some absolutes in relationships between people, and between people and their political authorities, that can become the substance of particular rights. Men and women have an obligation under divine law to worship God:

it becomes a human right that they should be allowed to do so by the laws and conventions of states. Human rights form an element of Natural Law theory, and as such enjoy long acceptance; they amount to a series of limitations of the power of organized society over subordinate social components. These rights are both individual, when proposed in the interests of the person, and collective when a social section, an institution, or an entire society claims, as a right, to order conduct in certain ways. Human rights ideology, which was familiar in the ancient world, has grown in modern times in correspondence with the accumulating powers of the collectivist state and as a recognition of internationalism. The problem with what are thought of as human rights is that they propose universal laws yet lack a means of achieving universal assent: what is claimed by one as a human right may be, and as a matter of record, is frequently, denied by another. Natural rights formulae which secure universal agreement tend to be so general in statement that they are exceedingly difficult to apply in circumstances of actual controversy.

The Church of England fully endorses the existence of human rights and calls upon its members to consider respect for them a duty of faith. But the Church also recognizes a danger inherent in any ideological structure in which the *rights* of humans, if emphasized without reference to the divine laws, may lead to an aggrandizement of human pride and the cultivation of an incorrect belief in human moral autonomy.

SOME ERRORS OF THE TIMES

Indifferentism. It is frequently now asserted that all religions have equally valid insights into the nature of the divine, and that inside the Christian Churches themselves any formulation of the Faith is as good as any other. This relativism is to be regretted, since the Church maintains the exclusivity of the Christian revelation in relation to other religious systems, and considers the guardianship of precise doctrine to be an essential if unhappily divisive obligation for those who would stand in apostolic tradition.

Reincarnation. Belief in serial existence is plainly contrary to the teaching and to the life of Christ — whose humanity was as complete as his divinity, and who ascended directly to heaven after his time on earth.

Spiritualism. The Church does not believe that, in normal circumstances, it is possible to have an articulate relationship with the dead. The Church itself exists in both time and eternity, and is the providential means by which a connection of prayer is maintained between people in the world and in the celestial society. Human sensation ceases at death, when the human identity fashioned for life in the world no longer has purpose, and the heavenly person, fashioned by faith during lifetime, is raised to judgement.

Ethicism. Morality, it is true, has no necessary connection with religion, and it is quite possible for a person to adhere consistently to secular ethical requirements which have no religious provenance. For a Christian believer, however, the moral life is a consequence of applying spiritual obligations; the moral structure of Christianity does not exist for its own sake, or as an essay in calculated hedonism, but as a fulfilment of the demands of living in the Kingdom of Christ. Jesus came explicitly for sinners — for those incapable of observing moral obligations in their own strength.

III

The Christian Life

PRAYER

Prayer exists when there is communication with God. The form necessarily derives from the language and images of the world, and prayer will show all kinds of diversity: it is always and inherently, however, an address to the Creator. Even silent prayer, or meditation, is articulate in the sense that the individual approaches God with a mind whose consciousness has evolved through learned knowledge and experience of the world which is verbal. God himself *speaks* to humanity — the scriptural record is one of verbal images. As the worship of God is the primary purpose of human life, so prayer is the means by which it is conveyed. Prayer is thus not a mere dimension of the Christian life but its very essence. And in this the life of Jesus himself is followed. Scripture, again, portrays the Saviour as forever in communication with his Father: in the synagogue, in the deserted places of Galilee, in the wilderness of Judea, in the Temple, when at a meal, in the agony of Gethsemane, on the Cross. Jesus also taught his followers the most perfect form of prayer. The Lord's own Prayer, indeed, which echoes preceding scriptural exhortations, is a complete statement of the nature of prayer — an ascription to God which acknowledges his holiness and begs incorporation into his great design; a petition for worldly sustenance; a call for a forgiveness which is to be shared with others; a life which is capable of resisting evil. Only one of these components of the Lord's Prayer, it may be noticed, is concerned with the physical welfare of the person — the means of staying alive, the very food we eat. The rest of the prayer relates to the sovereignty of God and the spiritual condition of the one who prays. This is in some contrast to the list of personal requirements that men and women are liable to make the centre of their own prayers — a catalogue of releases from various sorts of misfortune which, humanly speaking, are understandably at the heart of daily anxieties. But the Christian life encourages an education in spirituality, and it is of the nature of authentic spirituality that such initial preoccupations are transcended through the contemplation of the great majesty of God. It is not our desires but his greatness which prayer encourages us towards. Truly Christian prayer, therefore, changes over a lifetime from the one-dimensional petitions for welfare to commentary upon the weaknesses of the person as a spiritual being. The more the experience of the world, the more the wise person is inclined to recognize the frailty of human nature and the possessiveness of sin. There is no escape from ourselves except through an approach to the divine pity. Prayer for others, in fulfilment of the second of the two commandments summarized by Christ, is one of the important ways in which human welfare does, however, become a crucial dimension of Christian prayer. The love of neighbour is intended to receive real expression in acts which sustain the believer's life, but it is before that a petition for spiritual well-being. At the heart of Christianity is the conviction that men and women cannot redeem themselves; the grace of God, the goodness of his mercy, the free gift of his perpetual forgiveness, are the true deliverers. In praying for others Christians acknowledge the universality of sin, and the companionship which unites those whose intention is the achievement of the blessing of God's presence in their lives. This also joins the present world and its citizens to the celestial society, whose prayers for us are the sustaining culture of spirituality, and whose unending reality is described in Christian integration with the communion of the saints.

In its formal liturgical structures the Church provides a communal basis for prayer, a distillation of the spiritual wisdom of the centuries. The Church also encourages individuals to be inventive in evolving prayer which derives from personal experience and context. Each person can be fully assured that however inarticulate they may seem to be, or however slight their educational qualifications, God calls them to be themselves when they pray — and to be certain that all prayer is an identification with the life which God wills for us. The last point is crucial: properly directed prayer seeks to place the individual in the grain of providence. Its purpose should not be the fulfilment of earthly desires but personal acceptance of what God intends. Prayer is thus a prophetic undertaking. Each person tries to bring the kind of things he or she desires into correspondence with God's providential enhancement of the spiritual person: those things are then desired which form the education of the soul and create the durable qualities which are the very substance of eternal life.

Prayer needs also to be regular, for it is, like food for the body, the means by which spiritual health and religious vitality are provided. The more we attempt to communicate with God, and the more attentive we are to discerning the nature of his responses in the unfolding of the events which touch our lives, the more will trust in God's providence become habitual. Prayers at each part of the day consecrate life itself, and as Christians should be particularly conscious of the passage of time — as marking the transience of the earthly pilgrimage — the hallowing of commonplace experiences defines commitment to eternity. Jesus spoke figuratively of the spiritual life as being extinguished by rank growths (Luke 8.7); prayer is a kind of cleansing agent which clears each life by removing obstructions to clarity of Christian purpose. Those who enter the Kingdom of Heaven have received God with the simplicity of a child (Matthew 18.3).

CONFESSION

Our Saviour came into the world because men and women are sinners: this is the stark truth at the centre of Christianity, and it is unchanging. Jesus offered redemption, but the nature of humanity is still the same as when he walked in the fields of Galilee. The terrible fact of human sin produced the great sacrifice of the Cross, and men and women, incapable of procuring their own salvation, were released from the eternal consequences of their sins if they would acknowledge them and seek the forgiveness of Jesus. The message of Christ is about the redemption of humanity; the essential preliminary is individual repentance. The problem for people today is that they do not feel like sinners. To some extent this has always been the case. Neglectful of their duties, diverted by pleasures, overcome by their own appetites, the seed of salvation within them has in many cases always remained ungerminated. Modern people in the developed societies of today, however, experience a heightened insensitivity to their own corruption: so many features of the prevalent culture discourage a realization of the need for repentance. From the youngest age, now, people are taught 'self-esteem' rather than a consciousness of inherent tendency to moral error; they are assured that 'self-fulfilment' legitimately derives from their entitlements as humans. Lives are passed in quiet material self-indulgence — modern people expect to possess so much compared with their predecessors. They expect emotional self-indulgence, too — and are given it in daily exposure to television dramas. The series of emotional mood changes through which an individual may pass in a short space of time, in an evening of television viewing, is without precedent in human development. People are by nature very adaptable, and doubtless there are advantages to be derived from all this — an education in the experiences of a wider context for living, for example — but virtually nothing now stimulates a sense of personal worthlessness as a preliminary to repentance in the Christian sense. The practical encouragement of self-indulgence has replaced self-sacrifice as the most salient characteristic of modern culture. Against the values of this world-picture, however, the Church continues to declare its ancient message: Christ came into the world to save people because they are sinners, and all have sinned. Whoever does not agree with this will not respond to the call of Jesus. He is the Good Shepherd who knows his sheep by name and brings them into the safe enclosure where they are protected against the spiritual consequences of their wrong-doing (John 10.11). But first they must repent.

The liturgies of the Church provide general confessions where believers may publicly acknowledge their need for the grace of God's forgiveness. However familiar — even conventional — these exercises in contrition have become, they remain exactly what they purport to be: a confession of individual sin. Reception of the Lord's body in the Holy Communion is always preceded by confession and absolution. The Church also encourages regular examination of conscience in private, and assures each person that Jesus offers forgiveness to all who seek him in this way. Christ himself entrusted the forgiveness of sins to the ministers he appointed to teach in his name (Matthew 18.18). There is an ancient tradition of auricular confession made to a priest in private, who is then commissioned by Christ to pronounce forgiveness. This manner of confession is also practised by some in the Church of England. What is important for the Christian life is not the form or style of confession, however, but regularity. As our *natures* are not changed by the reception of God's grace, the liability to sin continues in all people even after submission to Christ. Growth in spirituality depends upon frequent acknowledgement of personal weakness and a practical acceptance that humans can never, in their own strengths, achieve salvation.

In contrast, therefore, to modern humanism, with its reliance on the moral autonomy of the person, and its overweening optimism about the capacity of humanity to order its own destiny, Christianity proclaims, as it has always done, the flawed nature of men and women. Called by God to share with him in the enfolding of the divine scheme, and to that extent endowed with reasoning and reflective faculties, each person is none the less estranged from God by inherent imperfections which need the constant attention which confession of sin provides. If prayer is the nourishment of the soul, confession is the means by which human reason is guided.

SELF-SACRIFICE

The denial of perceived personal advantage is not a feature of modern society. Under the guise of self-development, fulfilment, the expression of human instincts, and sometimes even of an inherent right to experience all that life can offer, men and women are inclined to relax restraint in the enjoyment of pleasures. Self-denial is not recognized as a virtue by those who deny themselves very little. Modern people, at least in the developed world, also possess so much. And possession promotes possessiveness: it feeds upon itself to foster a personal culture in which the individual begins to identify with what is owned or enjoyed. Ultimately, perhaps, humanity will become the victim of its own desires, and life itself will be transformed in the mass anxiety of those who will have become terrified of losing the material things they possess. Nor is it only — nor is it primarily — in material possessions that modern people exercise minimal restraint: in the use of time, and in the licence of emotional responses, men and women have now come to place entitlement above denial. Even some of the most basic human functions, like the nurturing of young children, have by some become regarded as an impediment to the development of a career or a brake upon the enjoyment of social pleasures. Yet the sacrifice of time is the necessary preliminary to all service, whether in the small courtesies and kindnesses which elevate humanity, almost by definition, from barbarism to civilized virtues, or whether in the social provisions, performed voluntarily, which help others to transcend disadvantages. The Christian life is a life of service, following the example and command of Christ himself.

The Church is concerned with the cultivation of a spirit of self-denial in its own adherents for spiritual reasons, as well as wishing to meet the ends of social service. The spiritual formation of individuals is enormously enhanced by the sacrifice of the time devoted to the service of others, and by the personal denial of some comforts and pleasurable pursuits as a deliberate discipline of the appetites. It is often said today that happiness is the chief purpose of human life: it is certainly often claimed as the most desired end. For a Christian, however, this can only be true in a very qualified sense. For the follower of Christ happiness as an end in itself can only be defined in a spiritualized manner; authentic Christian joy is the attainment of insights and states of being which are anticipations of blessedness. Happiness in the world is not incompatible with this — Jesus himself is recorded as enjoying social companionship (Mark 2.19) and as remarking on the joy derived, for example, from a simply human event like the birth of a child (John 16.21). But this is very far indeed from the modern attribution of happiness as the purpose of human existence, and of defining it in relation to the satisfaction of human appetites or the pursuit of sensations of pleasure or aesthetic sensation. Self-denial in such matters is an education of the soul. Extreme asceticism may be a vocation for some who seek the Christian life; for most, however, a measured enjoyment of some pleasures balanced against denial of some others begins to construct a ladder of perfection within the ability of every believer. In actual society some pleasures of the body are avoided because of the sanction of opinion, and some pleasures of the tastes and emotions because of their deleterious effects upon health: such restraints in response to

convention or good sense have their rewards, but in the Christian life self-denial is
practised for its own sake, as an essential step
in the pilgrimage of eternity. Jesus is a lover
of sinners, and everyone will fail in some
aspects of their essays in self-denial — they
can however, be assured of the sustaining
love of Jesus, in their failures as in their
successes. But not to make an attempt at self-
denial, on a daily basis, is to miss one of the
greatest, as well as one of the most familiar,
occasions of spiritual advance.

SUFFERING

To some it will seem a paradox that
Christians have, down the centuries, welcomed occasions of pain, and sorrow, and
various sorts of deprivation, as truly liberat-
ing. For they are in the process of over-
coming the world. Suffering provides the
contours of the spiritual life; it gives texture
to the option of faith. An existence of
uninterrupted repose, of permanent freedom
from pain — which appears to be the ideal
for life envisaged by modern hedonists, with

their goal of vacuous happiness — would not only produce featureless people, it would also promote lives without depth or transcendent meaning. The dignity of the person is tried and established through successive challenges. These will actually occur anyway, for the human record indicates very clearly that they are ineradicable, and that the utopianism of modern humanism is simply unrealistic. Christians are those who know how to turn misfortune to good effect, trusting in the design of Providence and the nobility of character which they achieve who confront suffering with confidence. The modern world is losing the sense of suffering as a vocation, and of vicarious suffering — spiritualizing the afflictions of others through the fellowship of prayer — as a ministry of Christian love. A culture which promotes the material welfare of humanity as its highest aspiration, and which regards men and women as morally autonomous, also regards suffering as the ultimate evil: it is an affront to the sovereignty of humans. People today often speak agnostically of 'the problem of suffering'. But there is no problem about it: pain is only an evil for those whose human vanity assesses men and women as entitled to exemption from the laws of the creation. Humanity is, materially speaking, inseparable from all other matter, and like all living creatures it is locked in an unending sequence of life and death, of interaction with other created things, of a need for sustenance, of physical attrition. In the secondary environment of human society people experience living in an interpretative manner: this adds to their pain because they are able to envisage ideal modes of existence which they do not have the means of delivering. For the wise this will be an advance in human understanding, and their reasoned reflection on their dilemma — as thinking creatures in a world which was not devised for their repose but for their labour — will stimulate the higher thought which is one of the glories of the human response to the existence of all things. God did not ordain unending serenity for the people he placed in his world. He created us for discovery, for advance in wisdom, for ultimate blessedness. He also endowed men and women with strong emotional responses, and it is another

Christian characteristic to recognize that passions need to be as disciplined as the physical impulses or as the cultivation of reflective thought. Where the emotions achieve priority over considered choice, learned moral precept, or spiritual sense, the human person is unbalanced. Where they are underdeveloped, on the other hand, there is a desiccating attitude to life which restricts access to a finer appreciation of the qualities God has made intrinsic to human social exchange.

To be reflective in a world where there is a serious mismatch between aspirations and possible fulfilment is to suffer. Here is an anguish which can be either destructive of the person or extremely fruitful. The Christian chooses the second course. It combines ordinary realism with what is known of God's purpose from the Scriptures and the Tradition of the Church. To the vocation of suffering the Christian also brings acceptance of worldly disaster — of the effects for humans of living in an unstable environment, of death and injury caused by natural phenomena, of sickness, of accident, of the misfortunes produced by chance. It is, again, human vanity which regards men and women as somehow entitled to exemption from the effects of these things. It is, indeed, one of the ways in which people are called by God to share in the divine scheme for life that they are, unlike the rest of the Creation, able to recognize these afflictions as 'evils'. For the supposed evils are, in reality, simply meaningless occurrences: it is the God-given endowment of reason and reflection which enables men and women to interpret suffering, and so to enter the higher realm of consciousness which exists beyond mere animal reaction. The articulation of suffering is an indication of the divine calling of humanity to share with God himself in the development of the earth. It is to rise above the merely worldly, and to be offered occasions of real understanding. So what is now conventionally perceived as an evil is really the intimation of higher instincts; suffering is the price to pay for wisdom, and happy are those who learn to turn it to that purpose. The contours of the spiritual life define the landscape of the soul, therefore, and the soul is educated through suffering into acceptance of reality. This is no barren fatalism, but growth through engagement with the world as it really is, and not as the wills of humans would wish it to be. Such is the divine pity, and the merciful love of God, that even the things which seem to cause us so much grief in fact furnish us with the means of attaining spiritual splendour.

WORK

St Paul wrote that if a man does not work neither shall he eat (2 Thessalonians 3.10). This observation followed an instruction to Christians to avoid idleness. In the biblical account of the origin of human society, labour followed the banishment of man and woman to the east of Eden, in punishment for their first sin (Genesis 3.23). Work, therefore, can clearly be said to be an obligation for Christians. Indeed, the workplace, after the family, is where the vocation of the Christian life receives its delineation, and what a man or woman does in working hugely assists total formation as a person. That is why, quite apart from the legitimate considerations of social justice, it is important that Christians see it as an obligation to seek to provide employment for those who are without work. Jesus himself, in a parable, suggested the unnecessary improvidence of the situation in which the unemployed remained idle in the market-place all day (Matthew 20.3). The Church upholds the dignity of labour, whether it is in productive or service work, or whether it is in the rearing of children and the maintenance of the home. Work is the means by which the material circumstances of life on earth become conducive to human development; it is also, in the cultivation of the mind through intellectual labour, an enrichment of understanding. The Church teaches that in all work, as in other social dealings, both individuals and collective managements should practise honesty, fairness, integrity, and unrestrained effort. It is work, as much as love, which elevates relationships between people, and provides opportunities of service and self-sacrifice.

THE COMMUNITY OF LOVE

Love of the brethren should be a primary characteristic of the Christian life, and those would indeed not be recognized as followers of Jesus who did not regard all people, whether believers or not, as their brothers and sisters. Yet observers in all ages have noticed a gap between this aspiration and the distressing realities of human associations — including the Church itself. As the very body of Christ in the world the Church should, of all human institutions, strive for perfection; but it is composed of flawed people who carry into the Christian life all the familiar corruptions of the world. The great miracle of religion is that God persists in a relationship with people like us, and that he entrusts the knowledge of eternal life to the keeping and extension of mortals. The Church of Christ was not founded for the virtuous but for sinners. Baptism into the new life of Christ procures forgiveness but it does not eradicate human corruption. It should therefore surprise no one that the history of the Christian Church, and the Church of today, demonstrate the divine paradox that the treasure is in earthen vessels (2 Corinthians 4.7), and that although the treasure stored up in heaven accumulates through the witness of individual lives, the lives of individuals in the world continue to be subject to the deprivations of moth and rust (Matthew 6.19). People behold the Church of Christ and expect to see the perfect society; what in fact they see is a community of sinners, a cross-section of the world. And that is exactly what Jesus willed for his followers. The Church is *in* the world, and its divine commission is to be of the world — not in its lowest state, but as the sinners who constitute humanity aspire to become. Saints are those who transcend their natures, which remain tainted by their sins, and yet who achieve a kind of spiritual heroism. They are still enveloped in ordinary human failings, however, and the company of the saints, the visible Church of public observation, consists of ordinary men and women made extraordinary not by their achievements or their insights but by their membership of the eternal society of those who are forgiven by Jesus. It is a society open to any sinner who will admit to sinfulness. The Holy Spirit preserves this assemblage of the spiritually frail in the certainty of truth; God leans towards the earth and hallows it with the promise of an everlasting destiny for those who love him.

Every Christian should strive, against natural inclinations, to make the Church more Christlike. No one, however, should have any illusions about the limitations of human attempts at perfection. The Church is a home for the imperfect, for those whom the conventional reject, or whose capabilities fail to satisfy the requirements of whatever moral injunctions prevail. And at the centre of its divine mission is Jesus, forever saying, as he said to his first followers, 'I have not come to judge the world, but to save the world' (John 12.47).

AUTHORITY

In the modern world both political and social authority have been successfully questioned, and some basic freedoms have resulted. Philosophical systems and theoretical propositions have also been subject to

fruitful scrutiny. But the authority of religious tradition is rather different in nature,
because although its doctrines and teachings
are necessarily expressed in language and
images which require revision with changes
in the encompassing culture, its essential
truths convey the direct — because revealed
— truth of God himself. The present
individualist *penchant* for personal selectivity
with ideas and belief-systems can therefore
be extremely destructive if applied to the
internal authority of Christianity. The *doctrines* of the Faith are true in all circumstances
and for all time, and critical scrutiny of them
is probably only appropriate over matters of
verbal clarity in altered social climates, or of
adjusted supportive illustrative material.
Moral teachings plainly need restatement to
produce realistic application — but it must
be restatement or reinterpretation, or the
inventive application of received principles
to novel situations, and not the adoption of
concepts alien to the original deposit of
truth. Religious traditions become overlaid
with all kinds of accretions over time, and it
is always necessary for prophetic insight to
decide how best to clarify the authentic

vision by the removal of unnecessary obstructions. The truth of Jesus Christ, however, is always the same, and it is for all people. No one should come to the treasury of Christian understanding in the belief that it can be legitimate to extract from it just those propositions which seem personally conducive. For Christianity is a seamless robe; its various teachings are all interdependent, and have a vitality and internal consistency which enjoin acceptance as an organic unity. Nor can it be right for individuals to import into the Christian tradition ideas which are foreign to it, and to attempt a personal conflation of favoured beliefs in the hope that compatibilities will emerge of themselves. These are, whatever their benign intentions, those who do not enter the sheepfold by the door but climb in by some other way — and are rebuked by Christ (John 10.1) The central truths of the Christian faith are exclusive. The modern world would hardly countenance individualist selection of some of the prevalent sacral values of the culture — the evils of racism, for example — and Christians would be unwise, and not good stewards of the mysteries of God, if they allowed their own sacred teachings to be decided by private option. The people of God are the body of the Lord in the world, and that unavoidably requires them to declare his truth in a unitary and complete way.

THE MERCY OF GOD

Nevertheless, the teachings of the Church are for all people, and not only for those capable of discerning ideas presented in a literate form, or who exist in particular cultures, or who are morally pure, or are conventionally regarded as religious. The Saviour himself delivered his truths to the fishermen of Galilee. He calls us to acceptance — not always to full understanding. The arms of Christ are forever extended to receive all who confess their sins and who respond to the supreme generosity of his forgiveness. The saints who have preceded every believer beckon from eternity to those who are hesitant in responding to the serenity of the love of Jesus. It should not distress anyone that not all the teachings of the Church fall at once into their conception of the perfect religious system. The truth of Jesus is greater than the immediate comprehension of men and women, and in itself meets their aspirations to a higher vocation for human life than the materialism of the age will allow. Spiritual formation is progressive. With each step those who try to love Jesus will discover how great is his love for them.